MULTIMODAL COMPOSING IN CLASSROOMS

Taking a close look at multimodal composing as an essential new literacy in schools, this volume draws from contextualized case studies across educational contexts to provide detailed portraits of teachers and students at work in classrooms. Authors elaborate key issues in transforming classrooms with student multimodal composing, including changes in teachers, teaching, and learning. Six action principles for teaching for embodied learning through multimodal composing are presented and explained.

The rich illustrations of practice encourage both discussion of practical challenges and dilemmas and conceptualization beyond the specific cases. Historically, issues in New Literacy Studies, multimodality, new literacies, and multiliteracies have primarily been addressed theoretically, promoting a shift in educators' thinking about what constitutes literacy teaching and learning in a world no longer bounded by print text only. Such theory is necessary (and beneficial for re-thinking practices). What *Multimodal Composing in Classrooms* contributes to this scholarship is the voices of teachers and students talking about changing practices in real classrooms.

Suzanne M. Miller is Chair, Department of Learning and Instruction, Graduate School of Education, University at Buffalo, State University of New York.

Mary B. McVee is Associate Professor, Literacy Studies and Director, Center for Literacy and Reading Instruction, University at Buffalo, State University of New York.

MULTIMODAL COMPOSING IN CLASSROOMS

Learning and Teaching for the Digital World

Edited by Suzanne M. Miller and Mary B. McVee

Routledge
Taylor & Francis Group
NEW YORK AND LONDON

First published 2012
by Routledge
711 Third Avenue, New York, NY 10017

Simultaneously published in the UK
by Routledge
2 Park Square, Milton Park, Abingdon, Oxon OX14 4RN

Routledge is an imprint of the Taylor & Francis Group, an informa business

Library of Congress Cataloging in Publication Data
Multimodal composing in classrooms : learning and teaching for the digital world / [edited] by Suzanne M. Miller and Mary B. McVee.
p. cm.
Includes bibliographical references and index.
1. English language—Composition and exercises—Computer-assisted instruction. 2. Creative writing—Computer-assisted instruction. 3. Language arts—Computer-assisted instruction. 4. Educational technology. I. Miller, Suzanne M., 1949- II. McVee, Mary B.
LB1576.7.M85 2012
808'.0420285—dc23
2011037145

ISBN: 978-0-415-89748-8 (hbk)
ISBN: 978-0-415-89747-1 (pbk)
ISBN: 978-0-203-80403-2 (ebk)

Typeset in Bembo and Stone Sans
by EvS Communication Networx, Inc.

For our children: Casey, Zachary, Jaden, and Lillianna
And the many children and teachers who never stop exploring

CONTENTS

PREFACE

When my (Mary's) son Zachary was a first grader in elementary school, he came home from school one day with a work sheet (truth be told, he came home with a great many work sheets!). But, this day the work sheet listed comprehension questions about the story *Grandfather's Journey* by Allen Say. This was a book that Zachary knew well. We had read it many times, seated side by side, his brother Jaden pointing his pudgy fingers over the evocative watercolor illustrations of steam trains, ships, mountains, and a boy and his grandfather. We talked about our own journeys not between Japan and America as in *Grandfather's Journey*, but between New York and China and New York and Montana, the homes that Zachary knew—the places where his grandfathers lived. This book that describes a young man's journey from his home in Japan and out into the world was in this way linked to our world and our home to the sights, smells, sounds, and feelings of China and Montana, to grandfathers and to travel.

It will probably come as no surprise that Zachary resisted completing the comprehension worksheet (truth be told, he often resisted completing such worksheets!). But this day, he seemed unusually agitated. In a voice that betrayed his frustration and exasperation at having to explain himself to yet another adult, he said, "Mom, we read the story at school. The teacher asked us the questions. We answered them. She *knooows* (stressed and drawn out for emphasis) we know the answers." He then paused and looked at me his mouth set firm for dramatic effect before delivering his final question: "What … is … the … point?"

What is the point? My years as teacher and parent assure me that Zachary is not the only child who has asked this question. While there are many ways to deconstruct this story, what I think as I write this now is how Zachary's sense of this picture book was not as a mere story with beginning, middle, and end or set of characters, plots, and settings. The story, as discussed at home, was a multimodal exploration—the colors, the images, the linguistic text—all worked together along with our discussions to bring a connected, embodied meaning to the story to places, sounds, sights, smells, and people. It was thus evocative of a world Zachary had experienced in a sensory way. In a school setting, Zachary was only required to address the story in the most basic way: What do you comprehend? Mind you, I am not arguing that comprehension is not essential; it is. Rather, I cannot help but wonder: Where is the disconnect when even a first grader questions: What is the point?

At present a declining percentage of graduating high school seniors find what they do in classrooms meaningful and useful to their lives and futures—a point that is not lost on me as my former first-grader is now a high school student. "What is the point?" many students ask.

As parents, teachers, and scholars this is a question we (Suzanne and Mary) take seriously within this book as do our chapter authors and the teachers with whom they have collaborated. Despite what we are doing well as teachers and in schools, we are too often missing opportunities to reach out and engage our youth from elementary to high school. *Multimodal Composing in Classrooms: Learning and Teaching for the Digital World* speaks to the ways in which we, as educators, might help encourage teachers and other educators to rethink literacy and literate practices to engage in what many have referred to as "new literacies"—literacies that go beyond linguistic texts to draw across the multiple modes that we make use of every day in our attempts to understand the world.

These new literacies do not set aside traditional literacies. Students still need to know how to read and write, but new literacies are integrated. They acknowledge the ways that students, and all humankind, make meaning across multiple modes that we perceive with senses. Meaning, thus, is not just viewed as what print text on a page says. Meaning is what is represented and constructed through image, sound, gesture, color, and so on.

For more than a decade New Literacy Studies (NLS), multimodality, new literacies, and multiliteracies have been addressed theoretically. This area of scholarship has promoted a shift in many educators' thinking about what constitutes literacy teaching and learning in a world no longer bounded only by print text. Many scholars have emphasized aspects of literacy, reading, and writing in what some call "new times"—times that are defined by the rapid onset of globalization, shifting information structures, and emerging technologies.

In contexts of unprecedented change in the digital world, these scholars address the need for schools to educate youth in ways that lead them to be competent within a digital global economy. Although theory is necessary (and beneficial for re-thinking practices), what have been limited in these discussions are the voices of teachers and students, and studies of changing practices in classrooms. There is currently a burgeoning movement to address this gap as scholars and teachers seek to publish portraits of classrooms at all levels of schooling where learners are engaged in new literacies practices and multimodal learning. This book provides detailed portraits of teachers and students at work in classrooms and draws from findings across classrooms and educational contexts to elaborate key issues in transforming classrooms with student multimodal composing, including changes in teachers, teaching, and learning. Authors in various chapters introduce much-needed perspectives into these portraits of classroom practice.

Multimodal Composing in Classrooms: Learning and Teaching for the Digital World makes the argument that education has an urgent need for multimodal composing in schools as a powerful, engaging tool for student learning for exploring science, history, and the English Language Arts even in environments of high-stakes testing. Teachers and students learn to interpret and appreciate poetry using digital multimodality as a process of exploration and a process of construction. Students compose digital videos to articulate the meanings they see enacted in a prominent author's story. Youth explore the deplorable legacy of racism, prejudice, and murder as they investigate the history of America's Jim Crow era. Media students consider how camera angle and camera distance play a role in understanding and representing a classic drama. Across the chapters, authors introduce readers to students, teachers, and classrooms that are vibrant, creative, and engaged. While not all is perfect and sometimes frustrations and limitations surface, it is clear across all these classrooms that literacy is more than print and that learning—no matter the level of the learner—has a point.

In addition to presenting portraits of learning in action, the principles derived from these research stories work together across the chapters to manifest *a theory of teaching for embodied learning through multimodal composing*. The six components direct attention to teachers' actions and interactions: teachers' efforts focused on (1) developing a new literacies stance; (2) initiating a social space for mediation of collaborative composing; (3) co-constructing a sense of felt purpose for students' multimodal composing; (4) drawing on and encouraging students to draw on their identities and lifeworlds; (5) making design elements explicit as meaning-making tools; (6) supporting embodied learning through students' translating symbolically with modes.

Across these stories we see the compelling rationale for changing what is possible in school. Our findings suggest that schools focus too much on the cognitive and treat students as though they only have brains and not bodies. In the studies where students and teachers had opportunities to compose their understanding of curriculum with "multimodal composing" they used images, gestures, sounds, music, movement to represent and communicate the meaning—and that changed how they experienced school and learning. We conclude that what we need is embodied learning for all, including teachers, as the essential educational focus in the digital world.

Acknowledgments

Our colleagues in the New Literacies Group (NLG) at the University of Buffalo (UB) helped us to shape our inquiries into New Literacies Studies that led—eventually—to our collaboration and this volume. Special thanks to Mary K. Thompson and Fenice B. Boyd who engaged in discussions on early versions of this work.

We are grateful to Donna Alvermann, who spoke to an admiring audience in Buffalo, visited the NLG, and generously hosted our trip to UGA for conversations that formed the beginnings of this book. Thank you for your support, your important work, and your wonderful hospitality.

When Mary Kalantzis and Bill Cope first came to the University of Illinois, Urbana-Champaign, they were gracious enough to drive around the lake to speak to an enthusiastic audience in Buffalo and consult on our projects. As assemblers of and key participators in the New London Group, they inspired our first interests in multiliteracies and have sustained our work with theirs.

We are indebted to Jim Gavelek whose interests in work related to embodiment, semiotics, and multimodality have influenced our writing in this text.

We acknowledge our graduate students at the University at Buffalo, actors in our local social networks who have enthusiastically pushed our thinking with their questions, their inquiries, and their multimodal texts, over time refining our New Literacies stance.

We are most grateful to the remarkable teachers represented here and the many others who have made the cultural jump to multimodal composing in their classrooms. Their courage, self-critique, and persistence in contexts that were not always supportive, embody the transformative attitudes that lead the way to new modes of learning.

The adolescent students in the classes of those teachers continue to inspire us with their eloquence and energy. Even in classrooms where their knowledge was not honored, they took up opportunities to engage body and mind in multimodal composing. When teachers supported their embodied learning, students came alive in school and thoughtfully put that experience into words from which we all might learn.

We owe much to Naomi Silverman for her enthusiastic support of this project and to our families, who suffered our absence (body and/or mind) as we made time to complete this book.

1

MULTIMODAL COMPOSING

The Essential 21st Century Literacy

Suzanne M. Miller and Mary B. McVee

A pre-service teacher downloads an image of Spiderman to her multimedia composition to make a pointed contrast with Walt Whitman's line of poetry and to build a metaphor about her life identity (www.multimodalpoetry.org). A pair of fifth graders consider how to use color and sounds to represent their knowledge about the environment and how acidic water in ecological systems affects living things. In an urban classroom, two 11th graders, Paige and Nicole, import the haunting song "Strange Fruit" by Billie Holiday onto the sound track of their movie trailer about Jim Crow Laws while they discuss whether National Archives images of lynching victims are too gruesome for the audience (http://gse.buffalo.edu/org/cityvoices/festmov/featured.php).

All of these students are engaged intently in making sense of the world and the curriculum through multimodal composing. In this book we tell the stories of these and other teachers and students engaging in such multimodal literacy through digital composing. Our purpose is to provide visions of classrooms where such new literacies become new tools for understanding and learning in school.

Why Multimodal Literacy?

Over the past 20 years, the idea of literacy has changed dramatically. The typical idea about literacy as reading and writing print text has expanded into multimodal literacy, which includes reading and writing multiple forms of nonprint "texts" such as images, web pages, and movies. Through producing and interpreting print, nonprint, and print-mixed representations in the digital world, people have developed new social literacy practices. Daily life now often includes use of Internet Web pages with images, voices, and music mixed with print. It is clear that in 21st-century social and cultural contexts, meanings are more and more represented *multimodally*—with images, sounds, space, and movement representing and communicating meaning (Kress, 2010).

How did such a revolution happen? As a "once in several centuries" innovation (Simon in diSessa, 2000, p. 3), the computer has been transforming our world and shaping new ways of making and using texts. Computer-based digital technologies provide new (and quick) access to these multiple modes of representation. The resulting digital world has influenced how all of us work, think, and live, creating a "new landscape of communication" (Kress, 2000, p. 183) marked by images at the *center* of our everyday experiences. Images are unlike print language; they are composed and need to be "read" with nonlinear logic. Arguing for an urgent change in school curriculum, Kress (2003) explains that language is a time-based, sequentially organized mode, while images are space-based and simultaneously organized; competence with mixing these modes involves design. Facility with *design*—the process of orchestrating representational modes and their interconnection—is therefore vital for composing a text that can meet the communication demands of new and future multimodal environments: "Design refers to how people make use of the resources that are available at a given moment in a specific communicational environment to realize their interests as makers of a message/text" (Jewitt & Kress, 2003, p. 17). As many texts are now widely created through images mixed with print and other modes or means of representation, the literacy practices needed for functioning in the world have been and still are rapidly transforming (Kress, 2010; Leu, 2002; McVee, Bailey, & Shanahan, 2008a; Miller, 2008; Miller & Borowicz, 2005).

This change is particularly significant for our students, who have grown up surrounded and shaped by literacy practices related to computers, the Internet, mobile phones and other ubiquitous computing devices for communicating, taking pictures and video, playing music and games, searching for and storing digital material. As a substantial part of youth culture, these everyday tools and texts bind children and adolescents in a social culture through continual communication and meaning making. Increasingly, the millennial generation (born after 1981) immersed in popular and online cultures, thinks of messages and meanings multimodally, rarely in terms of printed words alone.

Professional literacy organizations have concluded that such new literacies are essential to 21st-century learning (e.g., International Reading Association [IRA], 2001; National Council of Teachers of English [NCTE], 2003, 2008). One consensus policy statement (Conference on English Education [CEE], 2005) helpfully takes up these issues: It argues that multimodal literacies yield composed products that are "legitimate and effective" with the potential to be "more dynamic, interactive, generative, exploratory, visual and collaborative" than print alone. This statement emphasizes the importance of providing opportunities for *students* to engage in multimodal composing in school. For one reason, an expanded notion of text can provide them with opportunities "to reinvent and enhance notions of audience, purpose, genre, form, and context"—mainstays of the English Language Arts (ELA) curriculum—through multimodality. This book is grounded in the view of multimodal composing as a design-based means of both communicating *and* coming-to-know.

Throughout the chapters, we invite you to consider such changes in classrooms and to experience those changes in stories of teachers and students. Even in restrictive contexts of high stakes testing, teachers are introducing students to multimodal composing with a variety of outcomes that have included new levels of student engagement, content learning, and conceptual understanding. We turn first to the kinds of changes that teachers have made in their understanding of literacy and knowing in an effort to transform their teaching towards students' multimodal composing.

What Counts as Literacy and Knowing?

One important consequence of the intense abundance of knowledge in the digital age is the transformation of what counts as *knowing* (Lankshear & Knobel, 2003, 2006). The status of knowledge that already "exists" in statements (*propositional knowledge*) has changed: with the superabundance of digitally accessible information, no one can "know" all there is of importance to know in the world (e.g., currently the indexed web has almost 16 billion pages)! What has become essential is *performance knowledge*—knowing *how* to find, gather, use, communicate, and imagine new ways of envisioning assemblages of knowledge.

This dramatic change to "knowing as an ability to perform" (Lankshear & Knobel, 2003, p. 173) reflects a rethinking of what it means to know in an age where evolving social practices are aimed at gaining attention to one's point of view on collected resources. These "practices of knowing.... reflect a range of strategies for assembling, editing, processing, receiving, sending, and working on information and data to transform diverse resources of 'digitalia' into 'things that work'" (p. 173)—that is, composing new digital resources and multimodal texts with representational meaning and communicative purpose.

The ability to *design* such texts using multimodal resources to represent knowledge and communicate it for a purpose is now required for civic, personal, and workplace lives. For example, in creating flyers, signs, social network pages, videos, and other online content, images and print work together, often with other modes. Color, size, typeface, direction, spacing, movement, music, and other aspects of design represent and carry meaning. In digital practices outside of school, youth actively compose meaning through these new kinds of digital texts in their social worlds (Lenhart, Madden, & Hitlin, 2005). At the same time, in school, a declining percentage of graduating high school seniors (nationally only 28%) find what they do in classrooms meaningful and useful to their lives or futures (Bachman, Johnston, & O'Malley, 2008). These two intersecting 21st-century trends provide a stark image of changes we need to make in schools. Critiques of existing schooling point to the "more compelling and motivating" multimodal learning that students engage in outside of school (Gee, 2004) as an explanation for the increasing student disengagement in classrooms. Attention to this issue is central to the New Literacies Studies, which focus on these new kinds and uses of texts. Interdisciplinary educators and educational organizations agree that traditional schooling and literacy are not adequately preparing students for the 21st-century public, private, and workplace spheres (e.g., IRA, 2001; Kalantzis & Cope, 2008; NCTE, 2008; Partnership for 21st Century Skills, 2006).

There is general agreement, too, that the work educators and scholars are pursuing under the umbrella of New Literacies Studies is diverse, meaning many things to different educators (cf., Albers & Harste, 2007; Baker, 2010; Coiro, Knobel, Lankshear, & Leu, 2008; Lankshear & Knobel, 2003, 2006; Mills, 2010; Pahl & Rowsell, 2006). Varying approaches are essential to move the field toward a better understanding of the role of new and emerging digital technologies in teaching and learning. Next, we briefly situate this book in relation to work of others in the field in terms of theory, context, and participants.

How this Book Fits into New Literacies

The landmark publication of the *Handbook of New Literacies* demonstrates the importance of new literacies to the field. It also reflects that much new literacies research has focused on Internet-based technologies. To date, the majority of that work has been in reading and comprehension (e.g., Coiro et al., 2008), with much less work focused on interactive and composing processes. Given this prevailing focus, there is a need to explore the constructive and socially situated nature of meaning making related to the new literacies involved in composing with digital technologies.

Despite recent attention to digital literacies the literacy "field has tended to focus upon the individual(s) versus group(s) as the meaning makers" (Tierney, 2008, cited in Alvermann, 2009, p. 23). In contrast, the new literacies focus on the socially situated nature of literacies as an important aspect of meaning. Lankshear and Knobel (2003, 2006) draw from Gee and others who observe that "the focus of learning and education is not children, nor schools, but human lives seen as *trajectories* through multiple social practices in various social institutions. If learning is to be efficacious, then what a child or adult does *now* as a learner must be connected in meaningful and motivated ways with 'mature' (insider) versions of related social practices" (Gee et al. 1996, as cited in Lankshear & Knobel, 2003, p. 48, italics in original).

Other studies have investigated these social practices, particularly among adolescents in out-of-school contexts (e.g., Alvermann, 2002; Hull & Nelson, 2005; Hull & Schultz, 2001; Lewis & Fabos, 2005) or in relation to the influences of media on youth in general (e.g., Ito et al., 2009; Jenkins, 2009). While we agree with Alvermann and Eakle (2007) who have described the in-school/out-of-school binary as overly simplistic and unrepresentative of the fluidity of 21st century digital lives, there is still a need to document the learning and experiences of a broader range of students in school settings. In particular, the field needs to systematically explore student and teacher learning in socially situated group contexts where emphasis is not placed solely on individualized portrayals of learning. To address shortcomings in the field, we focus on socially situated multimodal composition in a variety of school contexts, exploring the use of digital, multimodal meaning making in elementary and middle grades, high schools, and university settings with a focus on the co-construction of knowledge.

In addition, it is not enough to merely document what teachers do or do not do in their classrooms. There are portraits in research and practice of teachers integrating Information Communication Technologies (ICT's) into their classrooms (e.g., Shanahan, 2006; Watts-Taffe & Gwinn, 2007); for teachers in these works, the focus is on technology integration rather than on new literacies embedded in social practices or the affordances of multimodal composing for teachers and learners. Others (e.g., Kist, 2004) have presented negative-case examples to demonstrate that teachers sometimes suggest they are doing new literacies, but it is just traditional school practice made over with a bit of gloss and glitter. There is a handful of work where practitioners and researchers have attempted to describe new literacies pedagogy in practice from a teacher's viewpoint, a learner's viewpoint or from both (e.g., Albers, 2006; Bailey, 2009; McVee, Bailey, & Shanahan, 2008b; Miller, 2007, 2008, 2010a; Pahl & Rowsell, 2005). However, there are, to date, still too few portraits of teachers engaged in new literacies practices, particularly those related to multimodality, and, at the same time, still too few portraits of students engaging in literacy learning through such socially situated multimodal practices in schools.

In all, our aim in this text is to contribute to the ongoing work in the area of new literacies in three important ways. We explore the socially situated nature of pedagogical practice by teachers and teacher educators and the participatory and socially situated learning of grades 5–12 students and preservice and inservice teachers. We present actual portraits from teaching and learning in school settings, often nested within larger research projects. In particular, we focus on the composition of multimodal texts in a range of school settings—from elementary children to inservice teachers enrolled in a graduate program. In so doing, we seek to explore the affordances and limitations of multimodal composing for 21st-century teachers and students and to extend new literacies research and practice in areas of significant need (e.g., see Tierney, 2009). To better understand the influences of teachers' attempts to include new literacies, we also address Moje's (2009) call for research documenting outcomes of new literacy practices in school, particularly how youth feel, if they are more engaged in classrooms, and what youth learn about content, about literacy practices, and about their identities and positions in the world.

Looking across the chapters in the book, we conclude that integrating the dramatic broadening of purposeful literacies and practices of knowing to include multimodal meaning-making systems beyond printed text for all students may be *the* essential task for schools in the 21st century (Miller & Borowicz, 2006).

The Promise and Problems of Multimodal Composing

The multimodal meaning-making systems available in digital multimedia texts include vast potential for designing linguistic, visual, gestural, audio, and spatial elements dynamically to communicate (Cope & Kalantzis, 2000, p. 26). Yet reviews of research illustrate a recurring problem with teachers' uses of digital technologies in classrooms—inattention to such multimodal design and to new ways of knowing (e.g., Leu, Kinzer, Coiro, & Cammack, 2004, p. 1600; Miller, 2008). In this volume we examine multimodal composing in the digital age as a significant way of making meaning and communicating, of engaging students and their audiences in purposeful representations of curricular concepts. The focus of the book, then, is particularly on using multimodal composing in classrooms as a literacy learning tool.

We recognize, as have others (e.g., Serafini, 2011; Unsworth, 2002), that changes in the digital age have not only influenced composition and products for digital literacies such as the web or e-books, but the use of images in traditional texts has dramatically increased as well. However, when teachers in teacher education classes and professional development workshops are faced with integrating images with print and other modes to compose multimodal texts into the contexts of their schools, impediments arise. Barriers to teacher integration of multimodal composing in schools can range from scripted-lesson classes and rigid curricula, to print-only values and test-prep-only mandates for the state graduation exam.

By reframing their purposes for their students' composing activities, though, teachers can design ways of integrating multimodal composing while also preparing for the state test (e.g., Miller, 2008, 2010a). They can offer students the opportunity to co-construct new purposes for school literacy (Miller, 2010b). These teachers who transformed their classrooms provide images of the kind of *New Learning* (Kalantzis & Cope, 2008) required for 21st-century personal, civic, and workplace spaces. In their framework for conceiving of teaching as a professional practice and education as a way of knowing the world, Kalantzis & Cope (2008) argue that

> Education in all its aspects is in a moment of change, or transition. The idea of "New Learning" contrasts what education has been like in the past, with the changes we are experiencing today, with an imaginative

view of the possible features of learning environments in the near future. What will learning be like, and what will teachers' jobs be like?

(p. 3)

This question about the future of education in a global knowledge society where learning happens everywhere (not just in schools) alludes to new tools, purposefully communicating with new media, and a balance of classroom agency with teachers acting as professionals and intellectuals facilitating "knowledge-making by learners" (p. 15) who are increasingly diverse.

These spaces designed by teachers can provide opportunities for students to create and perform their understanding. Students research; orchestrate music, narrative, images; create and dramatize voice-overs; and write and enact scenes in order to create effective texts from multiple modes into "things that work" for their purposes. Students take on roles as researchers, interpreters, writers, editors, and designers of meaning. They take up these literacy events and in doing so "reinvent and enhance notions of audience, purpose, genre, form, and context" (CEE, 2005). In short, "Living in a cyber world has transformed the very nature of literacy itself" (Alsup et al., 2006, p. 284). In response, we must prepare teachers (and they must prepare their students) for designing and interpreting multimodal texts for 21st-century lives.

To ensure teachers are prepared for the 21st-century digital world, teachers and teacher educators must take up the pressing issue of what constitutes effective pedagogies for multimodal composing. The design of the pedagogy needs to be central IF it is to guide teachers and teacher educators in creating 21st-century classrooms. The research-based chapters in this book tell stories of teachers designing and re-designing their teaching and of students taking up opportunities for multimodal composing in classes to make sense of the curriculum, themselves, and the world. These teachers and students struggle and sometimes succeed, providing lived-experiences that create a larger narrative about the problems and potentials for multimodal composing in schools.

An Overview of the Book

The book begins by focusing on ELA teacher learning and change with stories of teachers taking up 21st-century multimodal practices and developing new literacy goals for students. In chapter 2 Mary McVee, Nancy Bailey, and Lynn Shanahan discuss the responses of preservice and inservice teachers (K–12) to exploring digital technologies and literacies in a teacher education course. As teacher educators, the authors articulate some of the fears that surfaced as they began shifting their stance toward situated, social, and collaborative learning that is the hallmark of multiliteracies. They also share concerns raised by the teachers in the course, who sometimes expressed discomfort with new technologies and new literacies. Building on their own insights as teachers and on the insights shared from students in the course, the authors convey a sense of how learners (both teachers and teacher educators) progressed from equating new literacies with technical knowledge toward a more transactional approach of new literacies that emphasized multimodal design and composition.

David Bruce (chapter 3) takes up his experiences in learning to focus on the structures of multimodal texts, specifically of digital videos. He provides a detailed look at the "grammar" that structures video narratives and examines one teacher's storyboard and critical analysis of a professionally produced movie, *Henry V.* In unpacking the details of how the images, sounds, movements, and pacing of shots integrate to form the story, teachers learned to understand the complexity of multimodal design and the affordances of modes to encode meaning. Articulating their implicit knowledge to make it more explicit, teachers (and students) became aware of how they could use these modes to create intended meanings and powerful messages.

The question of whether these changes in teachers' perceptions carried over into their own classes is taken up in chapter 4. Nancy Bailey traces the experiences of an English teacher as she moved from a graduate class on new literacies (described in chapter 2) into her ninth-grade classroom. This story of Carol Olsen focuses on her changes as she tried to use new literacies and multimodal composing with students. At first she used these as "hooks" to engage students in the "real" work of reading print texts. In reflection on her students' responses and course readings, she gradually developed a "New Literacies stance," moving to new kinds of curricular activities to engage students in meaningful literacies that drew on their local knowledge (Bailey, 2006, p. 17). This account focuses attention to the process of learning to re-see multimodal composing as a literacy in the classroom and to provide opportunities for students' to link themselves to school and construct powerful literate identities.

In chapter 5 James Cercone portrays the classroom space created by a tech savvy teacher and shows how his students take up the opportunities for multimodal composing in a music video intertwined with their own narrative writing. His account of the daily practices of the Digital Video (DV) Workshop show how students engage in planning, writing, discussing, supporting, and composing with purpose and meaning. The teacher's role as executive producer and more experienced mediator emerges clearly in support of students' roles as readers, writers, collaborators and directors. A focus on Mercy's video *I Am A Revolution* provides an example of the influence such literacy experience can have on student engagement, learning, and identity-making.

Monica Blondell and Suzanne Miller (chapter 6) narrate the story of an experienced 11th-grade English teacher in an urban school that expected literary texts to be used as preparation materials for the state graduation test. As Diane Gorski introduced student composing of digital videos as a literature-learning tool, the preparation for the test was still central. During a series of four DV projects during the school year, her focus changed toward "meaning that matters" for students. A rethinking of literature in school marked the trajectory of her change, as she struggled to make DV composing projects work better for student learning. These activities revitalized literature interpretation for students and for herself, while also providing the felt aesthetic experience that had been missing. Focal students said that they finally understood re-reading text for a purpose to make sense of literature.

The story of a fifth-grade classroom (chapter 7) by Lynn Shanahan describes elementary school children using digital composing to develop and explain their understanding of acid rain. Following different groups of students as they composed their hyper-text slides, she uncovers differing abilities of students to design multimodal texts in ways that represent their understandings. This story of one class communicating with multiple sign systems provides lessons on multimodal composing as related to teacher-communicated beliefs about literacy and multimodal texts. Implications for professional development and teacher education include the need for explicit attention to the affordances and limitations of various sign systems and an expanded view of reading and writing.

Chapter 8 begins with a narrative of how students Nicole and Paige took up their teacher's invitation to compose digital videos as an inquiry into key concepts of American History. To provide a research-based guide to such integration of multimodal composing into classrooms, Suzanne M. Miller, Mary Thompson, Ann Marie Lauricella, and Fenice Boyd propose a "multimodal literacy pedagogy" as a framework for designing pedagogical change. The history teacher, Keith Hughes, redesigned his pedagogy to (1) create a supportive social space for mediation, (2) consistently construct felt purpose for embodied teaching and learning, (3) draw upon the identity and lifeworlds of students, and (4) provide explicit attention to and instruction in multimodal design. The elements of this framework are examined by drawing on the dynamics of Keith's classroom in which the digital video *For Colored Only* was produced by Paige and Nicole, with an emphasis on how the multimodal composing process influenced their learning.

In the final chapter, Miller and McVee synthesize the lessons learned from these stories of teachers and students attempting to transform themselves, their classrooms, and their learning. Reading across school contexts, subject-matter, grade-level, and varied means of multimodal composing, they propose key principles and issues for teachers and teacher educators as they work to reconceptualize literacy and engage students in 21st-century learning through multimodal composing.

References

Albers, P. (2006). Imagining the possibilities in multimodal curriculum design. *English Education, 38*(2), 75–101.

Albers, P., & Harste, J. (2007). The arts, new literacies, and multimodality. *English Education, 40*(1), 6–20. [Introduction to special issue.]

Alsup, J., Emig, J., Pradl, G., Tremmel, R., Yagelski, R. (with Alvine, L., DeBlase, G., Moore, M., Petrone, R., & Sawyer, M.). (2006). The state of English education and a vision for its future: A call to arms. *English Education, 38*(4), 278–294.

Alvermann, D. E. (Ed.). (2002). *Adolescents and literacies in digital world.* New York: Peter Lang.

Alvermann, D. E. (2009). Sociocultural constructions of adolescence and young people's literacies. In L. Christenbury, R. Bomer, & P. Smagorinsky (Eds.), *Handbook of adolescent literacy research* (pp. 14–28). New York: Guilford.

Alvermann, D. E., & Eakle, A. J. (2007). Dissolving learning boundaries: The doing, re-doing, and undoing of school. In D. Thiessen & A. Cook-Sather (Eds.), *International handbook of student experience in elementary and secondary school* (pp. 143–166). Dordrecht, The Netherlands: Springer.

Bachman, J. G., Johnston, L. D., & O'Malley, P. M. (2008). *Monitoring the future: Questionnaire responses from the nation's high school seniors, 2006.* Ann Arbor, MI: Institute for Social Research.

Bailey, N. M. (2006). Designing social futures: Adolescent literacy in and for New Times. Unpublished doctoral dissertation. University at Buffalo, SUNY.

Bailey, N. (2009). "It makes it more real": Teaching new literacies in a secondary English classroom, *English Education, 41*(3), 207–234.

Baker, E. A. (Ed.). (2010). *The new literacies: Multiple perspectives on research and practice.* New York: Guilford.

Coiro, J., Knobel, M., Lankshear, C., & Leu, D. (2008). *Handbook of research on new literacies.* New York: Routledge.

Conference on English Education. (2005) *Beliefs about technology and the preparation of English Teachers.* Retrieved from http://www.ncte.org/cee/positions/beliefsontechnology

Cope, B., & Kalantzis, M. (2000). Multiliteracies: The beginning of an idea. In B. Cope, & M. Kalantzis (Eds.), *Multiliteracies: Literacy learning and the design of social futures* (pp. 3–8). London: Routledge.

diSessa, A. A. (2000). *Changing minds: Computers, learning, and literacy.* Cambridge, MA: MIT Press.

Gee, J. P. (2004). *Situated language and learning: A critique of traditional schooling.* New York: Routledge.

Hull, G., & Schultz, K. (2001). Literacy and learning out of school: A review of theory and research. *Review of Educational Research, 71*(4), 575–611.

Hull, G. A., & Nelson, M. E. (2005) Locating the semiotic power of multimodality. *Written Communication, 22*(2), 224–261.

International Reading Association. (2001). *Integrating literacy and technology in the curriculum: A position statement.* Retrieved from http://www.reading.org/resources/issues/positions_technology.html

Ito, M., Baumer, S., Horst, H., Bittanti, M., boyd, d., Cody, R., et al. (2009). *Living and learning with new media: Summary of findings from the Digital Youth Project.* Cambridge, MA: Massachusetts Institute of Technology Press.

Jenkins, H. (2009). *Confronting the challenges of participatory culture: Media education for the 21st century.* Cambridge, MA: Massachusetts Institute of Technology Press.

Jewitt, C., & Kress, G. (Eds.). (2003). *Multimodal literacy.* New York: Peter Lang.

Kalantzis, M., & Cope, B. (2008). *New Learning: Elements of a science of education.* Cambridge, UK: Cambridge University Press.

Kist, W. (2004). *New literacies in action: Teaching and learning in multiple media.* New York: Teachers College Press.

Kress, G. (2000). Multimodality. In B. Cope & M. Kalantzis (Eds.), *Multiliteracies: Literacy learning and the design of social futures* (pp. 182–202). London: Routledge.

Kress, G. (2003). *Literacy in the new media age.* New York: Routledge.

Kress, G. (2010). *Multimodality: A social semiotic approach to contemporary commmunication.* New York: Routledge.

Lankshear, C., & Knobel, M. (2003). *New Literacies: Changing knowledge and classroom learning.* Philadelphia: Open University Press.

Lankshear, C., & Knobel, M. (2006). *New literacies: Everyday practices and classroom learning.* Philadelphia: Open University Press.

Lenhart, A. Madden, M., & Hitlin, P. (2005). *Teens and technology: Youth are leading the transition to a fully wired and mobile nation.* Washington, DC: Pew Internet & American Life Project. Retrieved from http://www.pewinternet.org/pdfs/PIP_Teens_Tech_July2005web.pdf.

Leu, D. J. Jr. (2002). The new literacies: Research on reading instruction with the Internet. In A. E. Farstrup & S. Samuels (Eds.), *What research has to say about reading instruction* (pp. 310–336). Newark, DE: International Reading Association.

Leu, D. J. Jr., Kinzer, C. K., Coiro, J., & Cammack, D. W. (2004). Toward a theory of new literacies emerging from the Internet and other information and communication technologies. In R. B. Ruddell, & N. J. Unrau (Eds.), *Theoretical models and processes of reading, 5th edition* (pp. 1570–1613). Newark, DE: International Reading Association.

Lewis, C., & Fabos, B. (2005). Instant messaging, literacies, and social identities. *Reading Research Quarterly, 40*(4), 470–501.

McVee, M. B., Bailey, N. M., & Shanahan, L. E. (2008a). Using digital media to interpret poetry: Walt Whitman meets Spiderman. *Research in the Teaching of English, 42*(3), 112–143.

McVee, M. B., Bailey, N., & Shanahan, L. (2008b). Teachers and teacher educators learning from new literacies and new technologies. *Teaching Education, 19*(3), 197–210.

Mills, K. (2010). A review of the "digital turn" in the New Literacy Studies. *Review of Educational Research, 80*(2), 246–271.

Miller, S. M. (2007). English teacher learning for new times: Digital video composing as multimodal literacy practice. *English Education, 40*(1), 64–83.

Miller, S. M. (2008). Teacher learning for new times: Repurposing new *multimodal* literacies and digital video composing for schools. In J. Flood, S. B. Heath, & D. Lapp (Eds.), *Handbook of research on teaching literacy through the communicative and visual arts* (Vol. 2, 441–460). New York: International Reading Association/Simon & Schuster Macmillan.

Miller, S. M. (2010a). Towards a multimodal literacy pedagogy: Digital video composing as 21st century literacy. In P. Albers & J. Sanders (Eds.), *Literacies, Art, and Multimodality* (pp. 254–281). Urbana-Champaign, IL: National Council of Teachers of English.

Miller, S. M. (2010b) Reframing multimodal composing for student learning: Lessons on *Purpose* from the Buffalo DV project. *Contemporary Issues in Technology and Teacher Education, 10*(2). Retrieved from http://www.citejournal.org/vol10/iss2/maintoc.cfm

Miller, S. M. & Borowicz, S. (2005). City Voices, City Visions: Digital video as literacy/learning supertool in urban classrooms. In L. Johnson, M. Finn, & R. Lewis (Eds.), *Urban education with an attitude* (pp. 87–108). Albany, NY: State University of New York Press.

Miller, S. M., & Borowicz, S. (2006). *Why multimodal literacies? Designing digital bridges to 21st century teaching and learning.* Buffalo, NY: GSE Publications & SUNY Press.

Moje, E. B. (2009). Standpoints: A call for new research on new and multi-literacies. *Research in the Teaching of English, 43*(4), 348–362.

National Council of Teachers of English. (2003). *NCTE position statement: On composing with nonprint media.* Retrieved from http://www.ncte.org/about/over/positions/category/media/114919.htm

National Council of Teachers of English (2008). *NCTE position statement: Definition of 21st century literacies.* Retrieved from http://www.ncte.org/positions/statements/21stcentdefinition

Pahl, K., & Rowsell, J. (2005). *Literacy and education: Understanding the new literacy studies in the classroom.* Thousand Oaks, CA: Sage.

Pahl, K., & Rowsell, J. (2006). *Travel notes from the New Literacy Studies: Instances of practice.* Clevedon, UK: Multilingual Matters.

Partnership for 21st Century Skills. (2006). *Results that matter: 21st century skills and high school reform.* Retrieved from http://www.21stcenturyskills.org/documents/RTM2006.pdf

Serafini, F. (2011). Expanding perspectives for comprehending visual images in multimodal texts. *Journal of Adolescent & Adult Literacy, 54*(5), 342–350.

Shanahan, L. E. (2006). *Reading and writing multimodal texts through information and communication technologies.* Unpublished doctoral dissertation, State University of New York at Buffalo.

Tierney, R. (2008). The agency and artistry of meaning makers within and across digital spaces. In S. E. Israel & G. G. Duffy (Eds.), *Handbook of research on reading comprehension* (pp. 261–288). Mahwah, NJ: Erlbaum.

Tierney, R. J. (2009). Shaping new literacies research: Extrapolations from a review of the *Handbook of Research on New Literacies. Reading Research Quarterly, 44*(3), 322–339.

Unsworth, L. (2002). Changing dimensions of school literacies. *Australian Journal of Language and Literacy, 25*(1), 62–77.

Watts-Taffe, S. M., & Gwinn, C. B. (2007). *Integrating literacy and technology: Effective practice for grades K-6.* New York: Guilford.

2

THE (ARTFUL) DECEPTION OF TECHNOLOGY INTEGRATION AND THE MOVE TOWARD A NEW LITERACIES MINDSET

Mary B. McVee, Nancy M. Bailey, and Lynn E. Shanahan

You may have decided to read this book because you are interested in using new literacies, digital technologies, or multimodal composing in your classroom. Like your students, you probably can't imagine your own life without digital technology. You use your computer to communicate through email and blogs, to shop for clothes and appliances, to find job prospects online, and even to map your route to important appointments or leisure activities. You use your digital phone to take pictures, store information, text, and talk to anyone from anywhere. Students in 21st-century classrooms don't know a world without the affordances of these digital technologies.

If you are like many of the teachers that we see in our pre-service and graduate courses, you may be excited about how to draw together your students' love for, need for, and dependence upon digital technologies with the literacy instruction that you provide. But, like many teachers you may also have questions about how to integrate digital technologies into your teaching; you may wonder about the "new" in "new literacies" or the implications of "multimodality." In this chapter you will meet students who are preservice and inservice teachers and some teacher educators (Mary, Nancy, and Lynn) who have struggled with these questions. In this chapter we explore some of the important aspects of new literacies and technologies and the questions, challenges, and learning that occur for our students and for us as teacher educators in the context of a new literacies course listed as "Literacy and Technology." This 15-week course met in a Mac lab once each week. Most participants were preservice and inservice teachers in graduate educational programs in Literacy and English Education. Throughout the chapter we attempt to trace some of the ways that we, and our students, have moved from viewing new literacies as merely technology toward a more complex and rich understanding of multimodality.

Similar to many other educators, our interest in new literacies really began as an interest in technology and literacy and in co-teaching a class titled "Literacy and Technology." We chronicled our initial adventures in a piece for teachers: "Technology Lite: Advice and Reflections for the Technologically Unsavvy" (McVee, Bailey, & Shanahan 2008a), so we will not repeat all of our observations here. As we have continued on our teaching journey, we continue to find that teachers do want to integrate technology into their teaching, but they are sometimes perplexed about how to do this in a truly meaningful way. While most of the teachers we encounter are increasingly proficient with emerging technologies in a personal sense, they have not readily integrated these technologies into their teaching or classrooms. Discussions and assignments have made us aware of this anecdotally, but we are also aware that survey results show that 53% of teachers do not routinely use technology (Zhao & Bryant, 2006) and even fewer teacher educators integrate technology into our courses (National Center for Education Statistics cited in Milken Exchange on Education Technology, 1999, p. i). We are also aware that though the number of computers and access to the Internet in classrooms have both increased significantly in the past ten to fifteen years (Snyder, Tan, & Hoffman, 2004), teachers still struggle to change their teaching strategies to include computer use in any significant way (Cuban, Kirkpatrick, & Peck, 2001; Pearson & Somekh, 2006; Walsh, Asha, & Sprainger, 2007). For example, Becker and Ravitz (2001) studied data from a national survey of over 4,000 teachers and found that some teachers did integrate computer technology into their lessons to provide exemplary instruction for their students, but the researchers conceded that this was occurring only among the statistically small proportion of teachers who had developed both technical expertise and also an understanding of how and why to integrate technology into their lessons. All of this research indicates that if you have been wondering if you were the only teacher out there still trying to jump the next technology hurdle, the answer seems to be that there are a legion of others still trying to figure out this "technology stuff," so you're in good company!

One of the particular challenges around technology is that as a quickly changing ill-structured domain (Spiro & Jehng, 1990), developing necessary expertise about technology and about implementing it can seem like a never-ending task. Elsewhere, Mary, our co-author, has compared a teacher's task of learning to use technology in classroom instruction to that of Sisyphus—"that unfortunate citizen of Greece who was sentenced to an eternity of pushing a rock up a steep hill only to have it roll down again and again," and concluded that "even integrating technology with teaching in basic ways, such as using literacy-related software or websites can be a perplexing task and *defies an easy lock-step approach* (McVee & Dickson, 2002, emphasis added, pp. 635–636). At this juncture, many teachers and teacher educators are in the same predicament. We realize that digital technologies and new literacies are important, even critical, yet we may be struggling with how to think about learning with new literacies in our classrooms (Honan, 2008). We may even wonder: Technology? New literacy? What's the difference?

In this chapter, we will share our emerging stance related to digital technologies, in general, and new literacies and multimodality, in particular. More importantly, we will share insights from our students who are preservice and inservice teachers as they have encountered new technologies and literacies that have acted as an impetus (albeit a sometimes frustrating one) for learning. We attempt to trace some of the developments in thinking from new literacies as technologies toward new literacies as embodying multimodal affordances—of which digital technology is a key element, but where mastering a technology is not an end in itself.

The Principle of Teachers First

As teacher educators we have grown along with our students as we have examined our own practices and positions to explore how we might integrate technologies and literacies in our teaching and in our students' learning. Our students engage in the same kind of reflection. This approach is closely tied to what Lankshear and Knobel (2003) refer to as the principle of "teachers first:"

> 'Teachers first' asserts the need to address teachers' needs in learning new technologies, and their relationship to language and literacy *even before* addressing the needs of students. For teachers to make sound educational choices about using new technologies in classroom practices they must *first* know how to use them (and any benefits of doing so) for their own authentic purposes. Teachers need support in making use of new technologies to enhance their personal work before learning to use them in their teaching.
>
> *(pp. 67–68)*

Ideally, the principle of "teachers first" positions inservice and pre-service teachers initially as learners who are allowed to experience and experiment with literacy and technology before they take on the responsibility of implementing these new technologies and literacies in their classrooms. We have learned in our own practice, as well as from watching the teachers in our class, that this step is critical, for it allows teachers time for experimentation and also for critical reflection on their experience. Through experimentation our students (pre-service and inservice teachers) *engage with* technology and literacy in new ways. Through reflection on their work in the course—work that focuses on both discussion of theory and hands-on experiences with integrative projects—the teachers themselves come to *think about* literacy and technology in new ways. These new ways of thinking and doing become the key to what we regard as transformative practice.

Many progressive educators have argued that teachers can and should learn alongside their students. To be clear, the principle of teachers first does not mean that teachers must only learn about technology in linear, lock-step fashion before attempting to teach. Rather such a principle represents the idea that teachers are an essential part of technology integration; teachers and their beliefs, comfort level, and learning should not be minimalized to one-shot technology training sessions. Teachers, in like manner to their students, need a supportive and transformative learning environment within which to experiment and explore. The principle of teachers first also posits that teachers should think of themselves as learners. Often as teachers, for altruistic reasons, we look to what new activities we can implement for students before we take that initial step back and ask: What have I learned? Where do I need to go in my teacher-learning? A focus on student-learning is, of course, essential for teaching, but the principle of teachers first encourages us to think about our own learning stances as teachers, that is, to think about our pedagogical content knowledge or when infused with technology what Mishra and Koehler (2008) have referred to as technological pedagogical content knowledge (TPACK) (see also Miller, Hughes, & Knips, in press).

Addressing the Fear Factor

Before our students can get to the point of transformation in their thinking, they sometimes have to overcome the fears and doubts they often bring with them to the class. It is very common in the first meeting of the course—and even afterward—to learn that the teachers taking the class are fearful about integrating technology into their teaching and doubtful that they can overcome the discomforts of a paradigm shift. Some teachers are uncomfortable about not knowing all the answers. Others are simply uncomfortable about working with technological tools that are not always predictable. As teacher educators, we have found that in order to get our students to make use of the "teachers first" principle, we have to help them to get past the fears with which they enter into the work of our new literacies course. You may find yourself with the same fears and doubts and may find it helpful to hear how many, even most, students overcome their fears. Additionally, there are number of teachers who dislike or are uncomfortable with other aspects of course literacy content.

Fear and loathing is a phrase some of our students have used in reference to content (e.g., poetry) and to technical undertakings (e.g., building a web page). For example, in the first major project in the course we asked our teachers to construct a digital multimodal interpretation of a poem they had selected. This project elicited anxiety from many of our students who told us that earlier experiences with poetry had not been pleasant for them. Deena's comments reflect a common dispositional stance:

> I am one of the many who have always feared and despised poetry. I remember having to read and write poetry in school and the anxiety that

> would come with each assignment. It was pretty similar to the sinking feeling I had when I read about this project. How am I supposed to interpret poetry when I cannot even pay attention to it long enough to get to the end of the poem? For this particular project I began to worry that I would never find a poem that I would connect with …

While the poetry project elicited anxiety that was directed toward course content, students' responses of fear and loathing were at other times a result of the technology itself. This was especially prevalent when students worked with software to create an inquiry-based WebQuest. Some students found the software or the unfamiliar Macintosh computer platform difficult to navigate. Students like Janie discussed the anxiety and frustration they experienced during the project:

> For starters, the technology was new to me. I am unfamiliar working with an iMac to begin with, so I already felt anxious. I was surprised how much more frustrating it was working with an iMac for this project than it was for the [earlier digital poetry interpretation]. I suppose this is because when you are working with something completely new and unfamiliar, it would be nice to be able to rely on your literacy with everything else, in this case, the computer. To my disadvantage, my unfamiliarity with the iMac only intensified my struggle with the … software.

Taking on New and Uncomfortable Stances

New or unfamiliar content and electronic snafus required the development and maintenance of new, and sometimes uncomfortable, stances, not only for students but for their instructors as well. We often found that we could not address all the dilemmas and challenges that arose or immediately master all of the intricacies of the software students were using. Our knowledge of the software was constantly being tested, in fact, as students thought of ever more complex ways to complete assigned projects. For example, as Laura wrote about the process of creating her WebQuest, she referred to one such test of her instructor's knowledge about software:

> I knew that I wanted to create something in the website that would make the cursor scroll down to the Introduction of the WebQuest when someone pressed the word "Introduction" at the top of the page. When Professor Bailey tried to help me, she filled in the hole. "You want to create an anchor," she said. This vocabulary word made all the difference. Although she couldn't tell me [immediately] how to create one, I was able to find this information in the Help section.

At first it was uncomfortable for us as instructors to respond to students by saying, "I don't know. I'll have to get back to you on that." Or to ask of other students, "Has anyone had this problem?" Or ask, "What is the best way to...." Shifting our stance from teacher as the dispenser-of-knowledge to teacher-as-shared-problem-solver was essential. In order for students to design complex, integrated projects, problems often required on-the-spot solutions and, typically, collaboration. Thus, successful teaching and learning at the technology/literacy interface required situated, distributed knowledge and the creation of alternative spaces, where this knowledge could be shared, accessed, and where new knowledge could be created. Gee (2003) says of this,

> The really important knowledge is in the network—that is, in the people, their texts, tools, and technologies, and, critically, the ways in which they are interconnected—not in any one "node" (person, text, tool, or technology), but in the network as a whole.
>
> *(p. 185)*

In an excellent example of the network to which Gee refers, the Help section of the software program became as important for solving Laura's problem with website construction as the knowledge that her instructor could provide. After putting together what she learned from both sources, Laura herself became an important extension of the evolving network; both her instructor and other students later consulted her about installing anchor links as she became the resident expert on this activity.

The students realized that when they integrated technology into their own classrooms, they too would face having to look less than fully knowledgeable in front of their students. Janie discussed this inevitability in one of her reflections when she contemplated a teacher's fear:

> The biggest challenge, I think, is going to be getting over our fear of relinquishing our personal control in the classroom as teachers. We are used to being the authoritarians and the leaders, the ones with the answers. In a classroom utilizing DV [digital video production], that role would be impossible to fill. A good teacher is confident enough to admit when he or she lacks all the answers and takes part with the students in the cooperative learning taking place. It takes courage and faith in what a project has to offer for a teacher to step down as the expert and embark on a unit that he or she is not completely familiar with. I like to think I have that courage, and I do have that faith in what DV has to offer.

Here, Janie clearly articulated a lesson learned from experiencing some of the frustrations that are part and parcel of working with technology in the classroom, but it is a lesson that we hope that teachers will apply not only when working with technology, but also in all their work with students.

There is a risk of failure in approaching teaching and learning in such a co-constructed approach. At times, as instructors, we worried about how students would respond if we did not immediately have an answer or if we, in turn, posed the question to our learning community for a response. The students had their own worries. Some were worried that they would not achieve the right outcome, sometimes spending a lot of energy to trying to discover what they thought we were "looking for." Being in uncharted territory where they were asked "What do *you* want to do? What meaning do *you* want to convey?" was an uncomfortable and often times, frustrating experience for students and for teachers. There were times when all of us yearned for a lock-step or formulaic approach toward literacy and toward technology—"Just tell me what to do, and I'll do it!" Terry expressed her need for more direct instruction and more time to work on her project as she reflected in writing about her WebQuest project:

> The end product of this project that my partner and I designed is very satisfying; however, it took a lot of time, energy and frustration to reach the end result.... Usually, when I have been asked to create something in class, I have been well-versed or introduced to the technology that must be used to create the product ... Because I am a person that is very visual who learns best by example, I had a hard time putting this WebQuest together without a lot of direct instruction, but I guess that is how the inquiry process is intended to work.

Terry expressed her frustration and lack of satisfaction with the final product of the WebQuest. She expressed a desire for a formulaic approach, outlining how to use the technology, and mastering it before being asked to deliver a high quality finished project. The focus on the process of learning and creating a WebQuest took Terry out of her comfort zone when it came to her technology knowledge. Up to this point in the semester, Terry had been well versed in the technologies presented and had presented powerful finished products, so being a non-expert was a new role for Terry, one that was uncomfortable.

Shared Knowledge and Distributed Learning

We admit that in our own position as instructors, it is often uncomfortable for us as well, and we worry that we may be failing some students by not providing enough direct instruction or that students will perceive us as less-than-competent when we say we do not have all the answers. We recognize an important parallel between the ways that we support one another as teacher educators and the ways that our students are learning to support one another in our classrooms. For example, Laura, who later became an expert on a particular aspect—the insertion of anchors, as described above—at first relied on a classmate sitting next to her to fulfill her desire for instruction in the technical aspects of the software's technology. Laura's classmate had previously taken a Web Design course and had experience using the predesigned web templates. Laura utilized the predesigned templates to provide her with more support. Laura described this influence in her WebQuest reflection:

> When Jill showed me the templates that she used, I realized a mistake I was making in creating my Web Quest and Website. There are many premade structures that can be used to help with the design process. It makes more sense to build upon previously made designs instead of re-creating what is already there. The templates are often better designed than what I could create. As I bumped along in my older model Chevette Website, I watched other students cruise by in their Ferrari and Cadillac model Websites. I realized the difference—their "information salary" was higher than mine. They had more knowledge of Website building which led to fancier sites. Jill showed me the templates she was using that enhanced her design. Other students had previous experiences in creating Websites. As teachers, we need to realize that students come from different "information backgrounds." Students should not be evaluated based on the appearance of their vehicle, but rather by how far they have traveled.

Through collaboration and distributed knowledge Laura sought scaffolds to support her use of the technology to avoid what she perceived as "failure"—a website that was not professional looking. Here, we see Laura emphasizing the finished product in her own work, even as she admonished teachers not to evaluate their students in this way. Like many students her fear of unfamiliar content and feelings of insecurity with the technology created apprehension and discomfort. In a world where she was used to knowing the formula to "get it right," Laura found she had to collaborate to share information and take risks. Interestingly, by the end of this project, Laura had made the connection that growth in student knowledge and competence when thinking about literacy and technology were more important in the class rather than the quality of the finished pieces.

Although we continually urge students to focus on the learning and thinking process, they often, and only naturally, express fears about encountering unfamiliar content and feelings of incompetence in regard to technology. Those teachers who, like Laura, can work through these dispositions are more likely to take risks in the confines of the course. Although empirical data outside the university setting is limited (e.g., McVee, Bailey, & Shanahan, 2008b), we are cautiously hopeful that once having taken a risk inside the university classroom, teachers will also be more likely to take risks in their own classrooms as they integrate technology and literacy and come to think of it as a transactional process rather than discrete entities.

Becoming Comfortable with Discomfort

"Learning," writes Gee (2003), "should be both frustrating and life enhancing" (p. 6). He might have added that the things we learn most from tend to scare us a bit too. This was certainly true of our own experiences of learning to integrate technology into our literacy teaching, and it is true for the teachers we work with as well. Those who learned to tolerate their initial discomfort elicited by assigned projects seemed to be the ones who grew the most. For example, Kesha described her feelings and fears in a written reflection related to her electronic poetry interpretation: "Prior to beginning this poetry project, hearing the word 'poetry' instilled feelings of fear, uncertainty, and boredom within me. In school, I avoided the yearly poetry unit by faking illness and tuning out the teacher's instruction." Kesha then wrote in detail about her poetry interpretation, the support and insights she received from others, the role of technological tools with which she grew increasingly comfortable, and her decision to write her own poem and represent it digitally. Throughout her description, she carefully catalogued her discomfort with technology and with poetry but also constructed and enacted a particular discourse for learning. Ultimately, Kesha observed that "crafting this digital poem has taught me a great deal about myself, poetry, and technology. It gave me a new way to express myself and provided me with a new and exciting way to teach poetry to my students."

Many other students, we find, express Kesha's excitement at finding a new avenue for creating literate discourse and, most notably, for overcoming an initial distaste for poetry. One of our other favorite conversion stories comes from Kathryn who wrote that she "loathed" poetry and that upon seeing a poetry project in the syllabus "almost dropped the class." Interestingly, Kathryn not only survived the required digital poetry interpretation project, she chose to do a second poetry interpretation as her final project. These testimonials from our students parallel experiences in our own teaching and learning where growth resulted from choosing challenge over ease, and they encourage us to continue to try to teach in new ways.

Investigating Literacy-Technology as Transactional Processes

Perspectives on Literacy and Technology

Transactional processes in technology and literacy refer to the ways that literacy is continually reconstructed by new technologies rather than a perspective that views literacy and technology as separate entities (Bruce, 1997). Many things we think of as related to reading and writing (e.g., books, pencils, paper) were the new technologies of their day. In attempting to create spaces for technology integration, we as teacher educators have struggled with how our teaching often reflects a dichotomous view of literacy and technology. Our students often struggle with the same issue. For instance, Sandy wrote:

> I believe that if we are to successfully incorporate technology in our classrooms, our views of literacy must change as well. Simply being able to read and write is not enough. Students must take the skills that they

> are learning and apply them on the computer. This application may be as simple as using a word processing program to type a paper or something as complex as a WebQuest. Regardless of the application, technology and its required skills must be present in the classroom on a daily basis.

Here, Sandy is separating reading and writing from technology instead of expanding the definition of traditional reading and writing to include multimodal texts created through technology. When Sandy says, "Students must take the skills that they are learning and apply them on the computer," she is still maintaining a stance that holds traditional literacies and technology as dichotomous entities. She is imposing traditional literacies onto an electronic environment, not integrating the two.

Transactional Perspectives on Literacy and Technology

In our Literacy and Technology course, we teach students about the transactional relationship between literacy and technology and the ways in which the social practices of new literacies are growing out of new digital technologies. We urge students to make those compelling connections that go beyond the basic, linear, and technological (see McVee et al., 2008b). While many of us focus on the computer as the tool, it is not just the computer that is important. Far more important are the insights and learning that arise during critical moments of metacognition about one's learning with and through the technology-literacy interface. In shifting their perspectives away from technology and literacy as separate elements, learners begin to understand that literacy and technology are transactional (Bruce, 1997). This is important because it shifts learners' focus away from operationalized computing skills (e.g., how to run a software program) toward the ways that particular technologies (e.g., software programs) can facilitate literacy learning. Kendra clearly expressed such an insight when, in a critical moment of metacognitive questioning and self-response, she wrote:

> I realized that I am not as literate as I thought I was. Yes, I can use the programs and do the things I mentioned above, but can I accurately read a multimodal text? Can I create one? I think true literacy is having the ability to be thoughtful and purposeful when using technology, not just being able to use the technology in a technical sense.

Every semester we find teachers who begin to question their own understandings of the technology-literacy interface. These students begin to understand (and often express quite dramatically) that reading and writing in a linguistic, print-based mode is not comprehensive enough for today's world. Through these epiphanies some students began to consider the notion that new and emerging technologies afford them opportunities to communicate multimodally. Like Jan, they begin to wonder what it means not only to act as consumers of multimodal texts, but as composers, or from a Vygotskian perspective, mediators, of such texts.

Bruce's notion of transactional processes in literacy and technology has helped us shift our own stance from a focus more on what Lankshear and Knobel (2006, p. 93) call "*technical stuff*" (digital technologies, software, hardware, and so on) toward the "*ethos stuff*" (a mindset of new literacies that focuses on how to take up and shape technology, or other tools, in particular ways: expertise is public and shared among many, performance is collaborative, learning is interactive and relational). Take a minute to look back over the first section of this chapter. We think that you will see that while we have included some aspects of this new literacies mindset (e.g., the principle of teachers first shared knowledge and distributed learning) by and large what we, and our students, emphasized was the technical knowledge. While acquiring technical knowledge can be a key step in developing a new literacies mindset—or that "ethos stuff"—a focus on technical stuff alone leaves us at the stage where we privilege the implementation of technologies as an end in itself. It is in this way, we argue that technology integration is deceptive. The end objective is not technology integration or even teachers using technology in their classroom pedagogy to deliver content—a "procedural" emphasis on technology (Miller, Hughes, & Knips, in press). Neither possessing technical knowledge nor integrating it into teaching is sufficient. Adopting a New Literacies stance involves adopting a shift in mindset and in teacher professional development, a focus on direct attention to the orchestration of multiple modes and more explicitly foregrounding of multimodality as a theoretical framework (Miller, 2008). In pedagogical terms, we are trying to implement in our own teaching what Miller, refers to as "Multimodal Literacy Practice" (Miller et al., in press) wherein teachers: "(1) design social spaces for mediating composing activities; (2) co-construct with students authentic purposes for these composing activities; (3) focus explicit attention to multimodal design and critique of multimodal texts; and (4) persistently open opportunities for students to draw on their identities and 'lifeworlds'" (Miller et al. in press). In our context, technology is a part of this practice, but not the end in itself. While we have alluded to some of these points earlier in the chapter, we explore them more fully elsewhere (see McVee, Bailey, & Shanahan, 2008c).

Learning the Importance of Multimodal Design and Redesign of Texts

Multimodal Texts

Design and Multimodal Redesign refers to constructs originally proposed by the New London Group (1996) to describe multiliteracies. Rather than viewing literacy in its traditional form as a print-based entity, a multiliteracies approach is multimodal. Such an approach includes, but is not limited to, elements of visual, auditory, spatial, and linguistic design. The New London Group (1996) bases their concept of a literacy curriculum upon the notion of Design. This Design, in turn, is based upon the idea that in our changing times, communication and information are conveyed, more often than not, through means that are multimodal—that is, through combinations of linguistic, visual, audio, gestural, and spatial signs and symbols—rather than merely linguistic (e.g., print-based) texts that presently dominate schooling. Addressing the importance of multimodality for life in the 21st century, Kress (2003) observes that the affordances of new media that arise from digital technologies have both accelerated and intensified the move from a monolithic view of literacy to a view based upon multimodal literacy practices. As Kress explains, this shift has occurred because "multimodality is made easy, usual, 'natural' by these technologies" (p. 5). As teacher educators who teach about literacy curricula, we must be cognizant of and teach about this shift from a monomodal, print-dominated literacy to one that is multimodal and often anchored in "digital epistemologies" (Lankshear & Knobel, 2003, p. 156).[1]

Teaching a Metalanguage of Multimodality

As instructors, we became increasingly aware that the pedagogy in the Literacy and Technology class needed to shift to reflect what we were learning about multimodality (e.g., Kress, 2003, 2010). We attempted to follow the advice of the New London Group (1996) to provide overt instruction about the affordances of the various modes that digital technology made available. We wanted, moreover, to teach our students about the power that they (and, in turn, their students) would have at their fingertips by making conscious choices to use specific design elements—such as visual, auditory, or gestural images—as they communicated and represented their ideas in multimodal texts. Nancy, our co-author, presented notes on: "Basic thoughts on Semiotics," and prepared a presentation about principles of semiotics in which we told our students, "Teachers of literacy must know that many types of signs represent meaning; they must become fluent in many modalities and teach their students to read all major modalities to be prepared for 21st-century work and life." We brought music videos and advertisements to class, and we used them in class exercises in which we asked our students to view them "with a semiotic lens." We discussed how the various modalities were contributing to the meanings that students constructed as they viewed various media.

Students who were still grappling with the demands of difficult assignments, like poetry interpretation, and the intricacies of the new digital technologies they were learning, were understandably overwhelmed at times by this new "layer" of content to learn. In an online conversation, Laura articulated this concern that was soon echoed by several of her classmates:

> This seems exciting, but at the same time overwhelming.... the visual, musical, and narrative elements of the project all need to be addressed to teach our students how to integrate them well in a project. Each of these layers has a "grammar" associated with it. Then we must also teach our students software/computer elements, social aspects of working together, and, not to mention, our subject matter.

Despite some of the reservations expressed, we were pleased to hear students talking about the "grammar" of design, even as we continued to work out Kress's deeper meaning. Most of all, we were thrilled when students like Emily expressed, in the same online conversation, the excitement—even feelings of liberation—that we were feeling at being given such powerful tools to use and pass on to students:

> I wonder if students have been unknowingly waiting for this moment to come—when we are able to participate in the mode of communication that is most interesting to us. When we are taught how we can communicate in this medium in an educated manner. All at once, teachers are saying, yes, the form of communication that you enjoy and that you know most of America connects with and enjoys is valid and open for you to also communicate your message with others. Students are ecstatic and entering the medium with a high level of proficiency because their skills have been passively honed for all of these years.

Elements of Text Design

Teachers can facilitate students' multimodal explorations by asking a set of questions and by teaching specific discourse needed by learners to articulate their multimodal representations. Our co-author Lynn posits that when constructing multimodal texts, teachers and learners need to ask themselves and others:

> (a) What can the design elements, visual, linguistic, or auditory, do to convey my message? (b) What are the limitations in using the various design elements to communicate my message? (c) How can I combine the use of the design elements to spread meaning across the modes when attempting to convey my message? And (d) how does the use of various design elements deepen meaning and presentation of knowledge?
>
> *(Shanahan, 2006, p. 155)*

By asking these guiding questions teachers and students have the opportunity to intentionally recognize sign systems beyond traditional print-based modes. Learners can thus be scaffolded to think about the independent and interrelated ways different design elements can function together to communicate a comprehensive message. In sum, these questions assist in developing an intentional use of design elements where students can plan, regulate, and evaluate their communication across multiple sign systems.

In this new context of multimodality, texts became something very different for some of the students. For example, Deena, who wrote about how much she "feared and despised" poetry before this project, wrote at the end of her project, "The poem that I worked with was transformed as I added a multimodal dimension to it. It became more powerful and more meaningful as I added each image and sound so that I was able to almost feel the poem." Not only did Deena find enjoyment of the poem that she selected to interpret, but she also found that the multimodal poetry presented by her classmates also led to an enjoyment that she had never found before in poetry:

> The presentations viewed in class were so successful in showing individual interpretations of poetry. While viewing the work of my classmates, I was finally able to enjoy poetry. I was able to see various interpretations and how the use of illustrations, movement, and sounds could enhance both the poet and the presenter's visions.... This project made it possible for me to enjoy poetry, something that no one else was able to achieve at any other point in my life.

Valerie expressed the same kind of appreciation for the power of multimodality in her reflection about her Design/Redesign process after she completed a project for which she had created an iMovie. Valerie wrote that she was pleased that she had learned "how to piece digital pictures together in a way to represent a story through a combination of visual images, written text, and audio formats."

For Deena and Valerie and other teachers like them, we have found that it is not just essential to provide opportunity to design and redesign texts using digital means; teacher educators must scaffold teacher learning. Scaffolding is needed to help learners understand the nature of multimodal texts—both how to construct such texts and how to talk about such texts (Bailey, 2006; Bearne & Wolstencroft; 2006, Hull & Nelson, 2005; Leander, 2009). Thus attention to both multimodal synthesis across design elements and attention to a metalanguage to discuss design elements is essential for reading and writing hybrid, multimodal texts (New London Group, 1996). When teachers were taught explicitly about the nature of multimodality and how it can be used to construct knowledge, they developed an understanding of the power of spreading meaning across multiple sign systems. As a result, they became designers of some multimodal texts and knowledgeable consumers of others.

Learning as Characterized by Computer Mediated Epiphanies: Technology and Literacy as Tools

The word "epiphany" has its origins in the notion of something divine, for example, the sudden appearance of a divine entity. Most of us do not associate computers or other technologies or even new literacies with the divine (although we cannot resist a passing reference to Saint Isidore, Patron Saint of the Internet). By *computer-mediated epiphanies* we refer to the moments of profound connection and reflection in our own and our students' interactions with literacy and technology. These are changes in thoughts, beliefs, dispositions, or actions related to literacies, technologies, texts, or content covered in the course that students or instructors identified as important changes in their thinking or learning.

One such moment occurred for us as teachers and researchers when we realized that we had been referring to students' work with poetry as "Poetry Power Points" emphasizing the technology and software used rather than calling them "Poetry *Interpretations*" which emphasizes the process of knowledge construction related to poetry. Such a shift might seem like mere semantic positioning, but a shift in discourse reflected a profound shift in our understanding. Whereas the previous referent "Power Point" emphasized the "technical stuff," the shift to the latter represented our growing internalization of the idea that "Technologies participate intimately in the construction of all literacy practices. They are not separate from texts and meaning making, but rather are part of how we enact texts and make meaning" (Bruce, 1997, p. 300). In other words, by re-orienting toward the text and the social practices associated with it (Lankshear & Knobel, 2006), we were taking yet another step toward the new literacies mindset.

Other rich examples of these realizations came from our students. For example, at the end of the course, Kendra wrote,

> Now I see that technology is not just a tool, but a way to find and create meaning. It is an understanding, not just a physical tool or appliance one might use.... I have realized that I am not as literate as I thought I was. Yes, I can use the programs ... but can I accurately read a multimodal text? Can I create one? I think true literacy is having the ability to be thoughtful and purposeful when using technology, not just being able to use the technology in a technical sense.

Kendra's questions reveal a shift in her thinking. Similarly, Jan wrote at the end of the semester about a shift in the ways that she had once regarded technology and literacy as two different entities:

> I think now I have a better understanding of what technology is, how it can be used, and how it should be used. Before, I saw technology as a tool, a means to an end. However, through the projects and discussions we have had, I see that the process is often more important than the end, or the product.... Furthermore, literacy involves both understanding multimodal products and being able to create meaningful multimodal products. These are skills I was not taught formerly and it was difficult for me at first to think in a multimodal way. Even though I am constantly

> bombarded with multimedia, I never gave conscious thought to it. I also have never really thought about the multimodal nature of technology. I experienced it subconsciously and understood it subconsciously, but I do not think I ever gave it deep thought. I have even created multimodal products before, but without the metacognitive awareness that I had while creating projects for this class. The projects we did challenged me to think about word meaning, sound, color, layout, genre, and rhythm. Knowing how to combine all of these aspects is what makes this type of literacy much more complex than traditional literacy. [For example], the idea of there being a visual grammar never occurred to me, but it is everywhere.

Kendra's and Jan's remarks are representative of many comments we have read in our students' papers and heard in class discussions. Technologies as cultural tools mediate and construct what literacy means and how we engage in literate practices.

In teaching the course, a tendency to compartmentalize literacy and technology is a common struggle for our students and for us as teachers. For practical reasons, the course is still listed in the university as Literacy and Technology, and this encourages us and our students to think, and often to talk, in compartmentalized ways. Even when we believe we have internalized the transactional stance, we may be faced by events that demonstrate our own limited understanding. For us as teachers and authors, one of these moments occurred around writing and analysis related to this very section of our chapter in which we refer to "computer-mediated epiphanies." While we feel that the phrase "computer mediated epiphanies" captures the essence of how students talk and write about their experiences, we suddenly recognized that our label positions computers (the technology) as more of a mediational tool than the social, representational, and multimodal literacy practices that students engaged in during the course!

In reality, it was not just the use of computers, but new ways of exploring, using, and creating digital texts that mediated the increased metacognitive awareness for students. It was not just the integration of technology, but rather, the combination of talk, reading, and embodied engagement that led to this point. In particular, both instructors and students in the course came to realize that the literacy processes enacted during Redesign projects, during the sharing of distributed knowledge through social interaction, and during discussions of new literacies theory were all extremely important for taming the technology, understanding the powers of multimodality, and constructing personal meaning.

In teaching the class, we attempted to expedite this realization by continually admonishing students to "think about the process," not merely the multimodal products they were producing. Through the *social process*, we tell students, they will come to new understandings (Vygotsky, 1978). In her reflective statement following the creation of her poetry interpretation, Kimberly demonstrated that she "got" our message:

> Look what creating a visual interpretation of a poem ... allows the students to be involved in: rereading text, making connections, discovering meaning, questioning the writer's intentions, using and integrating technology using multi-modal experiences, presenting a final product that they can take complete ownership of, and most importantly, learning from the entire process along the way.

Here Kimberly makes a connection between some of the skills required by students in her classes and how they could enact these skills in the context of an electronic poetry project that created multimodal texts. Kimberly's awareness addresses critics who suggest that teachers must choose between technologies bells and whistles on the one hand and content and skills on the other. As an informed professional, Kimberly alludes to some of the skills her students could use when creating an electronic poetry interpretation.

Learning With and Through Literacy and Technology

In the title of this chapter, we refer to the "(artful) deception of technology integration." The promotion of technologies to improve our lives and dramatically change schools and teaching through increased access to information is itself deceptive. Knobel and Lankshear (2006) remark that a fairly large group of studies now exist that describe the use of technology in school settings, but they argue persuasively that "Very little of this literature, however, describes anything that is significantly new so far as literacies and social practices are concerned." It is, rather, "old wine in new bottles" (p. 54).

What then is the "artful deception" in technology integration? Teachers often comment that employing new technologies in schools is motivating to students. If students are interested in content, for example poetry, that students would otherwise find less-than-compelling, adding technology to the mix can be a good strategy in arousing their interests; all teachers have likely used this method of duping students into real learning. However, this motivational edge alone is not enough. Once interested, it is our mission to take students beyond mere interest and engagement toward passionate construction of knowledge. When students come seeking technical expertise or information, we can provide this for them, but we must also offer them new ways of thinking, learning, and engaging to demonstrate that learning is not just about objectives and discrete knowledge readily measured, but ways of thinking, acting, valuing, and believing. Kalantzis and Cope (2008) state this persuasively when they write: "Learners become co-designers of knowledge, developing habits of mind in which they are comfortable members of knowledge-producing and knowledge-sharing communities" (p. 40).

Promoting such reflective stances and means for thinking is something that students can take with them beyond the confines of a classroom. Indeed, these new relational interactions that extend beyond classrooms are at the heart of new literacies. As such, teaching and learning new literacies through technology is more of an art—more about movement, creation, expression, and interpretation than about hardware and software. It is where we recognize the power of the tools at our fingertips, tools that let us create image, word, sound, and movement to convey powerful meaning beyond what is often expressed in traditional print-based forms. As powerful tools that create and integrate image, sound, and movement to create multimodal text, new technologies, and new literacies, can provide opportunity for teachers, teacher educators, and students to create powerful new interpretations and representations of lived experience and knowledge.

Note

1. In our class context technology is a curricular focus, but we acknowledge that while technology offers many multimodal affordances, neither multimodality nor a new literacies mindset require technology as an essential element (see Albers & Sanders, 2010; Knobel & Lankshear, 2006).

References

Albers, P., & Sanders, J. (Eds.). (2010). *Literacies, the arts, and multimodality.* Urbana, IL: National Council of Teachers of English.

Bailey, N. M. (2006). *Designing social futures: Adolescent literacy in and for New Times.* Unpublished doctoral dissertation, University at Buffalo.

Bearne, E., & Wolstencroft, H. (2006). *Visual approaches to teaching writing: Multimodality 5–11.* London: Sage.

Becker, H. J., & Ravitz, J. L. (2001). *Computer use by teachers: Are Cuban's predictions correct?* Paper presented at the 2001 Annual Meeting of the American Educational Research Association, Seattle.

Bruce, B. C. (1997). Literacy technologies: What stance should we take? *Journal of Literacy Research, 29*(2), 289–309.

Cuban, L., Kirkpatrick, H., & Peck, C. (2001). High access and low use of technology in high school classrooms: Explaining an apparent paradox. *American Educational Research Journal, 38*(4), 813–834.

Gee, J. P. (2003). *What video games have to teach us about learning and literacy.* New York: Palgrave Macmillan.

Honan, E. (2008). Barriers to teachers using digital texts in literacy classrooms. *Literacy, 42*(1), 36–43.

Hull, G. A., & Nelson, M. E. (2005). Locating the semiotic power of multimodality. *Written Communication, 22*(2), 224–261.

Kalantzis, M., & Cope, B. (2008). *New learning: Elements of a science of education.* New York: Cambridge University Press.

Kress, G. (2003). *Literacy in the new media age.* New York: Routledge.

Kress, G. (2010). *Multimodality: A social semiotic approach to contemporary communication.* New York: Routledge.

Lankshear, C., & Knobel, M. (2003). *New literacies: Changing knowledge and classroom learning* (1st ed.). Philadelphia, PA: Open University Press.

Lankshear, C., & Knobel, M. (2006). *New literacies: Everyday practices and classroom learning* (2nd ed.). Philadelphia, PA: Open University Press.

Leander, K. (2009). Digital literacies. In V. Carrington & M. Robinson (Eds.), *Digital literacies: Social learning and classroom practice* (pp. 147–162). London: Sage.

McVee, M., & Dickson, B. (2002). Creating a rubric to examine literacy related software for the primary grades. *The Reading Teacher, 55*(7), 635–639.

McVee, M. B., Bailey, N. M., & Shanahan, L. E. (2008a). Technology lite: Advice and reflection for the technologically unsavvy. *Journal of Adolescent and Adult Literacy, 51*(6), 444–448.

McVee, M. B., Bailey, N. M., & Shanahan, L. E. (2008b). Teachers and teacher educators learning from new literacies and new technologies. *Teaching Education, 19*(3), 197–210.

McVee, M. B., Bailey, N. M., & Shanahan, L .E. (2008c). Using digital media to interpret poetry: Spiderman meets Walt Whitman. *Research in Teaching of English, 43*(2), 112–143.

Miller, S. M. (2008). Teacher learning for New Times: Repurposing new *multimodal* literacies and digital video composing for schools. In J. Flood, S. B. Heath, & D. Lapp (Eds.), *Handbook of research on teaching literacy through the communicative and visual arts* (2nd ed., pp. 441–460). New York: International Reading Association/Simon & Schuster Macmillan.

Miller, S. M., Hughes, K., & Knips, M. (in press). Teacher knowledge-in-action: Digital video composing as 21st century literacy. In S. Kadjer & C. Young (Eds.), *Teaching English with technology*. Charlotte, NC: Academic Information Press.

Mishra, P., & Koehler, M. J. (2008). Introducing technological pedagogical knowledge. In American Assocation of Colleges for Teacher Education [AACTE] (Eds.). *The handbook of technological pedagogical content knowledge for educators* (pp. 1–29). Mahwah, NJ: AACTE and Erlbaum.

New London Group. (1996). A pedagogy of multiliteracies: Designing social futures. *Harvard Educational Review, 66*(1), 60–92.

Pearson, M., & Somekh, B. (2006). Learning and transformation with technology: A question of sociocultural contexts? *International Journal of Qualitative Studies in Education, 19*(4), 519–539.

Shanahan, L. E. (2006). *Reading and writing multimodal text through information and communication technologies*. Unpublished doctoral dissertation, University at Buffalo, NY.

Snyder, T. D., Tan, A. G., & Hoffman, C. M. (2004). *Digest of educational statistics 2003* (NCES 2005). U.S. Department of Education, National Center for Education Statistics. Washington, D.C.: Government Printing Office.

Spiro, R., & Jehng, J. (1990). Cognitive flexibility and hypertext: Theory and technology for the nonlinear and multidimensional traversal of complex subject matter. In D. Nix & R. Spiro (Eds.), *Cognition, education, and multimedia: Exploring ideas in high technology* (pp. 165–205). Hillsdale, NJ: Erlbaum.

Vygotsky, L. S. (1978). *Mind in society*. Cambridge, MA: Harvard University Press.

Walsh, M., Asha, J., & Sprainger, N. (2007). Reading digital texts. *Australian Journal of Language and Literacy, 30*(1), 40–53.

Zhao, Y., & Bryant, F. L. (2006). Can teacher technology integration training alone lead to high levels of technology integration? *Electronic Journal for the Integration of Technology in Education, 6*, 53–62.

3

LEARNING VIDEO GRAMMAR

A Multimodal Approach to Reading and Writing Video Texts

David L. Bruce

I stumbled across the concept of video grammar mid-way through my 11-year high school teaching career. Having taught both regular English classes as well as Media Studies courses, the intersection of the worlds of print and non-print often informed my teaching with those different modalities. I knew from my print composition training, for instance, that students would need frequent and guided practice with a variety of meaningful writing assignments. Their writing prowess developed over time. The same was true with their reading of print texts. Students needed guidance in grappling to make sense of a variety of genres and authors.

However, early in the teaching of my media classes, I did not provide that same sort of scaffolding to their reading and writing of video. I erroneously assumed that because most of my students were avid movie watchers, that they would be able to reproduce camera techniques when they composed videos. This did not happen. Most of my students used the camera in a similar fashion, setting up nearly all their shots from a medium distance with a horizontal centering of the subjects being filmed. They were not using the variety of camera angles and techniques available to them.

Once I started providing my media students with the same sort of reading and composing guidance I had provided to my English classes, students responded with quality results. Teaching them a basic grammar of video narrative form provided a common language for them to discuss film in ways that expanded beyond the "liked it/didn't like it" paradigm that often typified discussions of movies. In teaching that same grammar as a composition activity, the student compositions improved exponentially. Nearly all my students used the camera more purposefully and to greater effect than when I did not provide them the explicit training. The storage closet that housed all of our video productions stood as a testament for an anecdotal pre-test/post-test for students learning and using a functional grammar of video.

In this chapter, I will discuss video grammar as a structural form that can be considered from a reading and composition perspective. I begin with considering "grammar" in its print-based connotations before situating it in terms of video. After providing an overview of what video grammar is, I detail an assignment I use with classes along with a student example of the activity. I conclude the chapter with considerations of critical viewings and connections between reading and composing processes.

Learning from Print Grammar

Before examining the concept of video grammar, it will be helpful to contextualize grammar in its language traditions. Grammar, unfairly or not, has a negative connotation, especially when considered in ELA settings. Perhaps this is because of the tradition of assigning exercises that disconnect language from its working contexts as has often occurred in the form of isolated grammar worksheets or sentence diagramming activities.

When considering the concept of grammar, it may be helpful to delineate between the various kinds. Hartwell (1985) parses grammar into five different levels:

1. Grammar in our heads—This is the tacit and unconscious knowledge of how native speakers use language (p. 111).
2. Goals of science in linguistics—These are the "fully explicit descriptions that model the competence of a native speaker" (p. 114).
3. Linguistic etiquette—This level is not actually a form of grammar, but instead refers to how language is used in various social situations (p. 109).
4. Rules of grammar—These attempt to codify and teach grammar #2 as a set of school language rules, or what Hartwell calls "incantations" (p. 119). These rules become a prescriptive set of rules that were meant to describe.
5. Stylistic grammar—These are grammatical terms used in the interest of teaching prose style for use in teaching writing.

The level of grammar is important because each serves a different purpose. For example, Grammar 1 explains how speakers unconsciously use their native language. Grammar 2 codifies that language use in descriptive rules and structures. However, in terms of a speaker learning to communicate with the language, Hartwell (1985) states, "rules of Grammar 2 are simply unconnected to productive control over Grammar 1" (p. 115). Other researchers have come to the same conclusion. Lester (1967) found that "there simply appears to be no correlation between a writer's study of language and his ability to write" (p. 228). In his meta-analysis of studies of writing, Hillocks (1986) found that formal grammar instruction had no impact on student writing ability.

The kind of grammar that does help a writer is level 5, where a student "learns to control the language of print by manipulating language in meaningful context, not by learning about language in isolation, as by the study of formal grammar" (Hartwell, 1985, p. 125).

Such an example is Noden's (1999) concept of *image grammar.* He compares writing structures such as participles, appositives, absolutes, and others to brushstrokes a painter might use in his/her work. Noden advocates teaching these verbal brushstrokes through the use of visuals and examples of writing in order to read and compose. Students learn to use the brushstrokes within the context of their own writing.

Noden's (1999) image grammar is an example of moving away from considering grammar as an exercise in technical function to a practice of grammar as a *form*. Winterowd (1970) describes form as the "*internal set of consistent relationships* in any stretch of discourse, whether poem, play, essay, oration, or whatever" (emphasis mine, p. 829). Kress (2003) defines grammar as "the overarching term that can describe *the regularities of a particular mode* which a culture has produced, be it writing, image, gesture, music or others" (emphasis mine, p. 66).

An analogous case can be made in terms of video. Video activities focusing on the "internal set of consistent relationships" and "regularities of a particular mode" will help a student become more fluent with video. However, those highly specified video assignments dealing with issues such as lighting considerations, white balancing a camera, and using microphones that are taught with no connection to producing a video composition are akin to practicing decontextualized sentence diagramming activities. Those exercises do nothing to help the student make a more fluent composition. Why? Activities taught apart from their contexts of students' own work do not meaningfully inform their compositions. However, students studying a *grammar of form* in the context of their reading and composing video helps them gain control of using video language.

For the rest of this chapter, I will be addressing the video equivalent of Grammar 5, namely the grammatical structures and forms that can be used in the reading and composing of narrative video.

A Focus on Video Grammar

There are a number of excellent resources on the language of film containing rich descriptions of kinds of cinematic techniques and camera usage (Costanzo, 1992; Golden, 2001; Monaco, 1981). Nearly all of the conventions used in narrative film and video can be boiled down to a combination of three basic kinds of camera shots. Based off of the language Begleiter (2001) uses, the three types of shots that comprise narrative video grammar are establishing, reaction, and perspective shots.

Establishing shot: Sets the informational mood, giving viewers a perspective of the surroundings and settings of a scene

Reaction shot: The viewer is shown a character's face, seeing how he/she responds to a situation or scenario

Perspective shot: The viewer literally sees through the eyes of a character, perceiving what he/she is seeing.

The still shots in Figure 3.1 come from a short video of a young girl sitting down at the piano to practice. She plays the song, then, after she has done so, marks off her assignment, and then smiles at a job well done. The stills below represent the three types of shots included in the video. In this sequence, the *establishing* shot is of a young girl sitting at a piano, getting ready to check off a completion of a piano practice task. The second shot is a *perspective* shot, seen from her eyes, actually placing a check beside the assignment she has completed. The third is a *reaction* shot, as we see her face, smiling with satisfaction, at having completed her piano practice.

These shots do not form a prescriptive order of sequence, rather a description of their function. They are less important by themselves but are grounded in telling a story. Messaris (1994) states that when a viewer sees film images, "interpretation is driven by the narrative *context*, not the *code*." (emphasis original, p. 76). These shots create a scene that, when viewed in combination of their narrative sequence, appear as if they are happening in real time.

In this next section, I detail using video grammar with a class. After describing the scaffolding involved, I provide the assignment parameters, and a student example. The grammar of form I describe in this section is grounded in the sociocultural learning context of a classroom.

In introducing video grammar to a class, I will select a short clip from a film that has a minor narrative arc—intro to conflict, rising action, climax, resolution—and show the clip several times. The first viewing is to acclimate students to what is happening in the scene. For the second viewing, I will pause the clip at every edit and ask them to answer aloud what kind of shot it is. This public reading of the scene reinforces the practice of identifying what kind of video grammar the shot is.

For the third viewing, I will ask them to attend to the camera angles and audio cues. Again, I will liberally pause the clip to focus on camera placement (i.e., *how did they use the camera to film this?*). On this viewing, I will also ask

FIGURE 3.1 Establishing, perspective, and reaction shot.

students to detail what they hear as well. I ask questions pertaining to audio cues, such as, *what kind of music is playing in the background? What is the "feel" of the music? What kinds of sound effects do they hear?* I will then ask them how the combination of visual and audio cues creates an intended effect, to make the scene appear as if it is happening as we view it.

After we have viewed the scene, I will demonstrate another deconstruction using a student example of the assignment. I will show them the film clip, and then show the storyboards along with the written rationale the student provided. After that, I provide the video deconstruction assignment.

An Assignment to Focus on Video Grammar: Deconstructing a Video Text

I have found that the following exercise is an excellent combination of reading and writing video. The two processes are indelibly linked together here. The idea behind it is for the reader to become aware of a film clip's structural components and how those components are woven together to create a narrative scene. The reader then writes/composes the films images on a storyboard, in essence, re-writing the scene.

Video Deconstruction Assignment

You are to take 1 scene from a movie and break it down for its component parts. The point of this exercise is to closely read a scene, examining the parts that make it up (sound, camera, acting, etc.) to see how the parts make the whole better. As you complete this assignment, you most likely will be watching this scene multiple times. You do not need to do every one of the following, but please keep these in mind:

- name the establishing/reaction/perspective shots
- # of edits
- camera angles/camera work/camera movement (zoom, tilt, pan/combo)
- sound effects
- score
- acting/writing/directing
- lighting/color

For this assignment, you are to:

1. Describe what the scene is about (~1 paragraph),
2. Storyboard the scene. If the scene has 15 edits, you will need to sketch 15 panels. Don't worry about being perfect. Capture the essence or shape of the visuals. If a scene repeats, simply indicate it on your storyboard by referring back to the previous storyboard panel.

3. Underneath each storyboard panel, list the type of shot being used (establishing/reaction/perspective—or combo of the 3). List any particular camera shot you notice. Also note any sound/music cue.
4. Write *how* the film is put together makes the scene work. In other words, how does the combination of types of shots, camerawork, and sound create meaning in the scene? (~1–2 paragraphs).

Before detailing the assignment, I find that it is helpful to provide additional scaffolding. For teacher education courses, I encourage them to select a film that they already use—or would plan to use—with their classes. That way, they are enacting a close reading with a film text with which they are familiar. In addition, they see a value in working on an assignment that has direct curricular ties. This can also become a model for their students.[1] To that end, I encourage them to make their scene selections appropriate for the 7- to 12-classroom setting. In addition, the scene should have a clear narrative story arc (beginning, middle, end) that lasts approximately between 30 seconds to two minutes.[2]

The assignment is accessible to nearly every kind of classroom setting because it does not require a high level of technical expertise or technology access. It is multimodal in that there is the visual and audio of a film clip, the drawing representation of the film's images, as well as the written analysis of the scene.

The following example (Figure 3.2) comes from a high school classroom

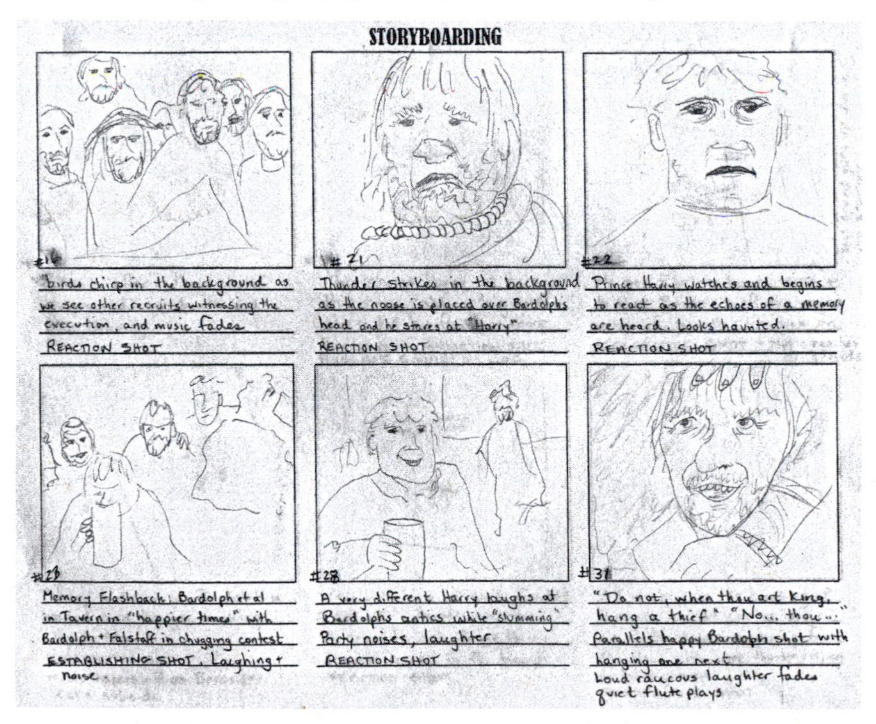

FIGURE 3.2 Excerpt of Teacher Deconstruction of *Henry V*—Storyboard.

English teacher, Jennifer, who used a scene from Shakespeare's *Henry V* directed by Kenneth Branagh. Notice in the storyboards that the teacher has indicated the kind of shot used as well as audio cues.

The following is the teacher's written summary of the deconstruction. Following the scene summary, she details how the visuals and audio interact to create an interpretation of the scene.

A Sample Deconstruction

> *SUMMARY*
>
> *This scene is an important scene in the play and the film, establishing King Henry as all grown up and taking necessary responsibility. It has been previously shown that "Hal" has been, before becoming King, a bit of a playboy, known to "slum" it with some of the local characters, Jack Falstaff, Bardolph, Pistol, and Mistress Quickly, to name a few.*
>
> *In this scene, Hal and his ragged band of volunteer soldiers are marching through France, and he is confronted with the necessity to make one of the hard choices that leaders must make: he must order the execution of Bardolph, former friend and ally, who has stolen items from a church. He must do so face to face with Bardolph, which makes the decision all the more difficult.*
>
> *DECONSTRUCTION*
>
> *Branagh seems to have chosen to shoot this scene very much focused on the two characters involved, King Henry and Bardolph. The scene, made up of a total of 49 individual shots, is comprised mainly of reaction shots, showing "Hal" and Bardolph caught in a heartbreaking situation. The camera's job seems to be to capture the emotion on each character's face, including those of the other men, in reaction shots where they are watching the event, designed to discourage any further looting. We are caught up in the King's personal "battle" between duty and sense of loyalty, and the scene's flashback sequence serves to underscore this inner struggle by showing us "Hal" and Bardolph in happier times, drinking and having fun. We are then jolted back to the present, where that happy Bardolph has been replaced by a ravaged, desperately sad Bardolph with a noose around his neck. The emotion escalates as the King, in tears, gives the order and Exeter kicks Bardolph's legs off the wagon, and Bardolph's body is raised into the air via the noose by some soldiers. Branagh takes the focus momentarily from the character's faces to the context, when we see a perspective shot of the King watching as Bardolph's body kicks and then is still, hanging from the tree. Branagh then returns the camera to the King's face, where we see his resolve to be an example to the men he is leading into battle by reminding the men of the consequences if they do not follow his orders to respect the French as they march toward Agincourt. Our last shot in the scene changes the camera angle entirely, as the camera is placed below Bardolph's body as it swings on its noose in a perspective shot that spotlights the Kings' words.*

The use of sound and music was interestingly coordinated; sound is used to punctuate moments, such as thunder rolling in the background, or birds chirping in an ironic cheerfulness as Bardolph is about to be hanged.

Branagh uses sound, distorted by echo, to foreshadow the start of a flashback sequence as the King and Bardolph gaze at one another, leading into the King's memory of the Tavern scene. No music is used during this flashback; only the sounds of laughter and happy hooting and hollering are heard during the main part of the flashback sequence.

Music is used only twice of note; at the end of the Tavern scene, the laughter and merrymaking fade to a lone flute plays quietly, foreshadowing an ominous end. Music also begins as the King is made to recognize Bardolph, and goes in and out, until the moment the King nods to Exeter to kick Bardolph from the wagon; a deep bass note sounds, beginning a frenzied crescendo that fades as Bardolph's body is raised, kicks, and then ceases to move. At the very end of the entire scene, after Bardolph is hanged, we hear only the creaking of the hangman's rope and the rolling of thunder, getting nearer and nearer.

Through a deconstruction of this scene from *Henry V*, the teacher attends to the video grammar: reaction shots "where they are watching the event," a perspective shot "of the King watching as Bardolph's body kicks," and establishing shot "of Bardolph's body is raised into the air via the noose." In addition, she pays careful attention to various audio cues such as "thunder rolling in the background or birds chirping" as well as careful placement of sparse background music. All of these multimodal elements come together to create a scene that highlights "King Henry as all grown up and taking necessary responsibility."

Reading Critically

The film critic, Pauline Kael, once pleaded with English teachers that as movies became more accessible in the classroom, they would not do to films what they had done with books. One of the problematic considerations I have had with this assignment is that it is, in essence, a reading of film in the New Criticism tradition. This assignment focuses on the literary techniques of film and how those techniques come together to create meaning. I bring this issue up with my teacher education classes when we do the activity as I want them to attend to not perceiving this as the only way of reading films. There are two issues dealing with reading films in this tradition.

The first is that, for most of the students and teachers with whom I have done this assignment, this is their initial foray into any cinematic language. With any textual readings, there should be attention to the available design (see New London Group, 1996) of the modality involved. This activity does that. Though the assignment focuses on the "literary devices" of film, at the core this is a close reading activity, a vigorous interaction with the text. Such a reading does not need to occur with every film text in brought into the classroom. Messaris (1994) warns, "Learning to understand images does not require the lengthy period of initiation characteristic of language learning" (p. 39). I have found this to be the case with this assignment, in that it only needs to be done once for students to be able to attend more closely to video grammar.

The second reason for doing this assignment is that a deconstruction opens doors for more critical readings. By examining the construction of the film, "readers" tend to ask questions about how editing decisions with visuals and audio can lead a viewer toward a particular interpretation. For example, I have used two films, *Fahrenheit 9/11* and *Fahrenhype 9/11*, that deal with the videotape recording of President Bush reading to elementary children while he is informed of the 9/11 terrorist attacks. Both films manipulate the footage to come to polar interpretations: indecisiveness and fear in one case, and command and control in the other. Through examining the cinematic devices, the reader can critique how those elements have been manipulated to lead toward a particular effect.

In addition, when using films in conjunction with print texts—such as the above example with the Branagh version of *Henry V*, or even comparing more than one cinematic treatment of a scene such as any of the numerous film versions of *MacBeth*—issues arise such as what the director chose to include, exclude, highlight, background, etc., which can open up any number of critical readings.

I have also used commercials in deconstruction activities, as the commerce and representational aspects of these narratives come to the foreground. Key questions aimed at critical readings of media texts (Thoman & Jolls, 2005) are useful in such viewings:

- Who created this message?
- What creative techniques are used to attract my attention?
- How might different people understand this message differently from me?
- What lifestyles, values, and points of view are represented in, or omitted from, this message?
- What is the message being sent?

These questions are great prompts for pushing the conversation to a critical analysis.

I have seen over the years that those students who are more astute viewers—having working vocabulary of video grammar and techniques—tend to read professional models with a more informed eye than those who have not had explicit training. This is an example of what Emig (1977) called first-order (talking and listening) and second-order processes (reading and writing). "First-order processes are acquired without formal or systematic instruction; the second-order processes of reading and writing tend to be learned initially only with the aid of formal and systematic instruction" (p. 122). The deconstructions allow students to acquire second-order processes of reading and writing video that they would not have learned without the "systematic instruction." I have observed numerous student reflections to this activity, stating that learning video grammar has foundationally changed the way in which they perceived narrative video.

Reading and Writing Connection

Deconstructing video is a multimodal example of how reading and composing are intertwined. Scholes (1985) states, "reading and writing are complementary acts that remain unfinished until completed by their reciprocals" (p. 20). Scholes (1989) clarifies that connection by stating, "we can write only with what we have read, and we can read only by writing" (p. 7).

This deconstruction activity focusing on the grammatical form of video, paired with composition activities, make for more astute readers and composers of video. As viewers become more aware of production elements, they are able to incorporate those elements into their own compositions. For example, in one of my high school media classes, a production group wanted to create a video in which the whole piece was one continuous camera shot. In planning their production, they read a number of music videos and film clips that had complex and extended camera movements. These readings informed techniques that they were able to incorporate into the composition of their own video. I have observed countless times where students will mimic techniques they have learned from professional media, reading video in order to write it.

Learning a language has to do with practice. Britton (1982) stated:

> Production of … written forms relies, of course, on knowledge of the written code itself, the formation of letters, words, sentences. How this is picked up … remains something of a mystery though two governing conditions seem likely: *a context of manipulative play* and picture making, and the association of this *learning with the purpose of producing* written stories.
>
> ([emphasis mine], *p. 65)*

Students need this same sort of manipulative play with video reading and composition, molding it, experimenting with it and shaping it with the eventual aim of telling some sort of story.

In every context in which I teach video composition, I begin with video grammar as a compositional guide. Having classroom participants think in terms of their own videos being comprised of establishing, reaction, and perspective shots provides them with a visual framework through which they can compose. Students may not be able to articulate the variety of cinematic devices, but they can replicate these three basic camera framings. Moreover, as they consider the narrative aspects of their video, they can use this grammar with intentionality and for effect.

Conclusion

In an interview, film director James Cameron (Gross, 2010) was asked what were influential films for him. He said that he watched Stanley Kubrick's *2001: A Space Odyssey* 18 times. He indicated that, as a fan of science fiction, he watched the movie six times in order to try to figure out what the film meant. However, he kept viewing the film because he wanted to know how the film was put together, and then he started experimenting with a camera and models to re-create the effects from the film. This was the point, he observed, where he made the jump from film viewer to film director. Our students most likely will not become Hollywood directors, but the example is clear. If we want our students to use video as a composition tool, they need a language to help them read it as well.

Hartwell (1985), in discussing grammar, introduced the term COIK, "clear only if known" (p. 119). The conventions of film allow for densely layered visuals, effects, texts, and/or sounds. These multimodal texts can only be read and composed when there is a clear knowledge of those conventions. Video grammar is a step toward that clarity of understanding.

Notes

1. I also make the entire class's responses available in an online format so that they will be able to have access to a number of potential classroom examples.
2. Commercials are also great sources of narrative sequences. They tend to be highly visual and are brief for classroom examples.

References

Begleiter, M. (2001). *From word to image: Storyboarding and the filmaking process.* Studio City, CA: Michael Wise Productions.

Britton, J. (1982). Spectator role and the beginnings of writing. In G. Pradl (Ed.), *Prospect and retrospect: Selected essays of James Britton* (pp. 46–67). Montclair, NJ: Boynton/Cook.

Costanzo, W. (1992). *Reading the movies: Twelve great films on video and how to teach them.* Urbana, IL: National Council of Teachers of English.

Emig, J. (1977). Writing as a mode of learning. *College Composition and Communication, 28,* 122–128.

Golden, J. (2001). *Reading in the dark: Using film as a tool in the English classroom.* Urbana, Il: National Council of Teachers of English.

Gross, T. (Producer). (2010, February 18, 2010) James Cameron: Pushing the Limits of Imagination. *Fresh Air.* Podcast retrieved from http://www.npr.org/templates/transcript/transcript.php?storyId=123810319

Hartwell, P. (1985). Grammar, grammars, and the teaching of grammar. *College English, 47*(2), 105–127.

Hillocks, G. (1986). *Research on written composition: New directions for teaching.* Urbana, IL: National Council of Teachers of English.

Kress, G. R. (2003). *Literacy in the new media age.* London: Routledge.

Lester, M. (1967). The value of transformational grammar in teaching composition. *College Composition and Communication, 18*(5), 227–231.

Messaris, P. (1994). *Visual literacy: Images, mind and reality.* Boulder, CO: Westview Press.

Monaco, J. (1981). *How to read a film: The art, technology, language, history and theory of film and media.* New York: Oxford University Press.

New London Group. (1996). A pedagogy of multiliteracies: Designing social futures. *Harvard Educational Review, 66*, 60–92.

Noden, H. (1999). *Image grammar: Using grammatical structures to teach writing.* Portsmouth, NH: Heinemann.

Scholes, R. (1985). *Textual power: Literacy theory and the teaching of English.* New Haven, CT: Yale University Press.

Scholes, R. (1989). *Protocols of reading.* New Haven, CT: Yale University Press.

Thoman, E. J., & Jolls.,T. (2005). Media literacy education: Lessons form the Center for Media Literacy. In G. S. P. Brown (Ed.), *Media Literacy: Transforming curriculum and teaching. The one hundred fourth yearbook of the National Society for the Study of Education, Part 1* (pp. 180–205). Malden, MA: Blackwell.

Winterowd, W. R. (1970). The grammar of coherence. *College English, 31*, 828–835.

4

THE IMPORTANCE OF A NEW LITERACIES STANCE IN TEACHING ENGLISH LANGUAGE ARTS

Nancy M. Bailey

When it comes to stances, many topics come to mind. Athletes, for instance, take stances. In fact, one merely needs to access a video sharing site like YouTube to learn how to strike an effective bowling, batting, or golfing stance. Surfers too, apparently, can benefit from assuming the proper stance. One can also take a political stance, a philosophical stance, and even a defensive stance—the last, being both physical and psychological. A stance, then, is a posture held either by the body or the mind. When located in the latter site, it is the result of beliefs and assumptions, perhaps even a product of long-time practice.

Several years ago, in response to the growing influence of Information and Communication Technologies (ICTs), Bertram Bruce (1997) pointed out that the new, digital technologies have fundamentally altered the nature of literacy, and he questioned the stance that those who teach literacy should take in relation to these new technologies. After an analysis of the various stances assumed by individuals who see technology and literacy as separate and autonomous entities and who teach literacy accordingly, Bruce rejected such stances and concluded that literacy and technology exist in a transactional relationship, with technology being "part of the continual reconstruction of literacies" (p. 303).

The implications of ideas like Bruce's (1997) for literacy teaching have been significant. Now, the debates about whether or not to include digital technologies in our ELA curricula are diminishing. Fewer and fewer people need to be convinced that digital technologies—as well as all aspects of new literacies—provide important tools for students' learning. Likewise, the strong relationship between literacy and technology (Bruce, 1997, p. 197) seems to be an ever more commonly held belief among literacy instructors.

As the discourse about literacy shifts, what literacy *is* seems to be increasingly well theorized, but *how*, specifically, teachers should teach new literacies is still not entirely clear. Lewis and Chandler-Olcott (2008) note the dearth of research literature that could guide teachers' understanding of specific instructional practices related to new literacies, and they call for more attention to this area. Indeed, we find many anecdotal accounts of individual classroom activities inspired by theories of new literacies (e.g., Cohen & Meyer, 2004; Kadjer, Frey, & Fink, 2006; Labbo, 2004; Seglem & Witte, 2009), but too little discussion about exactly how teachers can be guided to systematically create a new literacies curriculum. In this chapter, I address this issue by narrating the story of Carol Olsen, a ninth-grade English teacher, who gradually assumed a new literacies stance—a move, I argue, that is essential for establishing new literacies curricula and classrooms where students learn to use literacy in meaningful ways as they construct identities as confident, literate beings.

A New Literacies Stance

When I speak of a new literacies stance, I refer to the positioning taken up by a literacy teacher as she attempts to integrate new literacies into her curriculum. A new literacies stance is built upon a solid foundation of theory—especially theories of multimodality (Kress, 2003; Miller & Borowitz, 2006) and multiliteracies (New London Group, 1996; Walsh, 2009)—as well as deep knowledge of teaching and learning principles associated with sociocultural and constructivist approaches that are "active and critical" (Gee, 2003, p. 4). Thus, a new literacies stance must be firmly grounded in teaching strategies that emphasize dialogic and collaborative construction of knowledge, inquiry-based learning (Owens, Hester, & Teale, 2002), and guided participation (Rogoff, 1995) as well as multimodal consumption and production of all types of texts (Lankshear & Knobel, 2007). This stance must guide teaching and learning if secondary literacy instruction is to be effectively redesigned (New London Group, 1996) to meet the needs of 21st-century students.

An effective new literacies stance, moreover, also calls for the development of an "insider mindset" (Lankshear & Knobel, 2007, pp. 10–11). That is, teachers must do the kind of thinking and doing that their students who are "insiders" (Lankshear & Knobel, 2007) or "digital natives" (Prensky, 2001) engage in regularly. It is well documented (e.g., Alvermann, 2002; Bean, Bean, & Bean, 1999; Chandler-Olcott & Mahar, 2003; Gee, 2003; Hull & Schultz, 2002; Lewis & Fabos, 2005) that many students engage in far more sophisticated literacy practices outside of schools than inside. Unfortunately, too many teachers fail to familiarize themselves with the kinds of new literacies that their students regularly utilize in their blogs, text messages, digital movies, video games, or other forms of online practices. Some teachers do not recognize these practices as literacy events.

Thus, these teachers, with their outsider mindsets, cannot draw upon the rich thinking and well-developed knowledge—what Street (1994) calls "local knowledge"—that their students can bring to classroom practices. Without an insider mindset, Lankshear and Knobel (2007) claim, teachers cannot expect to offer consistently meaningful instruction to their students, partly because they do not understand the ways in which their digital native students learn best and partly because they don't know that new literacies are, and will continue to be, what their students need for future work, leisure, and lives as citizens (Kalantzis & Cope, 2008; New London Group, 1996; Walsh, 2009).

A teacher who does not develop her curricula from a new literacies stance may add activities to lessons that call for multimodal activity and the use of digital technologies into classroom practice, but if these are not systematically integrated with other sociocultural approaches and framed within a deep understanding of how to use principles of multimodality and multiliteracies (Kress, 2003; New London Group, 1996), then teachers may merely use what they think are new literacies to make more palatable to their students the learning of a static, anachronistic curriculum (O'Brien & Bauer, 2005). When teachers think that integrating new literacies merely means using digital technologies to engage and motivate students in disconnected activities while maintaining a largely "outsider mindset" (Lankshear & Knobel, 2007, pp. 10–11) and a monologic, teacher-centered curriculum, they may fail to create change in their traditional, static, classroom routines and miss opportunities to initiate significant growth in students' literacy experiences (Bailey, 2006). In contrast, the story of Carol Olsen demonstrates how a teacher who assumes a new literacies stance can create a dynamic learning space where her students can daily construct literate lives for themselves.

Multimodality as the "Spoonful of Sugar"

I first met Carol Olsen when she was a student in graduate classes at the university where I was teaching (see McVee, Bailey, & Shanahan, this volume). When she was enrolled in a new literacies class in which I was a co-instructor, but not the instructor who graded her work in the course, Carol agreed to allow me to observe in the ninth-grade classroom where she was teaching so that I could see how the new ideas about literacy that we were both learning could translate into classroom practice.

When I first observed Carol's English 9 class in early September, I was very impressed at how much multimodal composition and embodied learning she used in her lessons. For example, she had her students learn literary elements—authorized curriculum for ninth-grade English classes in her district—by finding irony or conflict in the song lyrics of popular music, by watching an episode of the television program, *Friends* to analyze the way elements of a short story were presented, and by acting out skits created to portray protagonists and antagonists or elements of foreshadowing. Carol filmed their skits and edited movies which the students reviewed and analyzed.

Soon after these early lessons, from about mid-September to mid-October, however, Carol reverted to very traditional methods to teach a unit of short stories, using round robin reading, teacher-centered discussions, and traditional worksheets where the students used factual knowledge in rote fashion. Her students approached these traditional learning tasks with compliance, but seemed not to have the enthusiasm and absorption that they exhibited when engaging with the multimodal activities during the first two weeks of school. Carol was disappointed, moreover, when many students did poorly on three very traditional quizzes that she gave to test how well they were learning literary elements, parts of short stories, and specific factual information about the stories they were reading.

Interpretation of Carol's reasoning for reverting to such traditional methods after such a propitious beginning to the school year came from analyzing both Carol's written reflections in her graduate class and also from her statements in interviews. Carol's lessons during the early part of the school year seemed heavily influenced by the ways in which she understood the nature of literacy and also by the way that this understanding informed her teaching. While she thought it was important to include digital technologies and other expressive media, like music, in her literacy lessons, she still considered these elements as separate and dichotomous when comparing each with print literacy. She was asked in the first meeting of her graduate class what she hoped to accomplish by taking the course, and she wrote, "Use more technology effectively *and enhance student literacy by using technology*" (emphasis added). Here, Carol seemed to consider literacy and technology as separate, rather than "a mutually constitutive relation" (Bruce, 1997, p. 303)—a view that signals a more complex and sophisticated understanding of how literacy and technology together can exist in a transactional and integrative relationship (McVee, Bailey, & Shanahan, 2008).

Additionally, she seemed to assume that by using "technology" (meaning computer technologies, and also television, music and film), students would be more likely to learn with and about printed texts because technology is often engaging and motivating for students: "Getting freshmen to become engaged, interested and excited about something, especially reading and writing, is an extremely difficult task. However, by incorporating technology *I have found a way to 'hook' them and keep them 'on the line'* for the rest of the year" (emphasis added). A week after she wrote this, when I asked Carol how she felt that her use of technology enhanced student learning, she again used the same metaphor to tell me about the motivational impact of technology, which she tied to her plans for covering required curriculum elements:

> From a student viewpoint, I think that [technology] is a motivator.... It not only piques their interest, but I think it makes them want to get more involved in the activity and learn more.... I think you hook them with

> the technology, and once they are engaged, it keeps them … Like, next week, I'm going to start literary terms, which, you know, they hate that … everyone hates that. But I'm going to teach it through music. Even their music, they have characterization, they have a plot, and they have a theme.… And then when I start my short story unit … well, I show a sitcom. Your sitcom has all this. Then they're ready to read the stories and it keeps them [motivated].

Clearly, Carol intended to use her considerable creativity to develop multimodal activities primarily to "hook" students, priming them for the traditional lessons in authorized print knowledge that would follow. Used in this way, the multimodal activities were more akin to "the spoonful of sugar to make the medicine go down" (Kist, 2005) than to new literacies instruction that draws upon significant learning principles (Gee, 2003) and is located in students' local knowledge.

The irony is that Carol's students did not appear as motivated to participate in class once she started the short story unit as they were when she was using the nontraditional methods built around multimodal activities. Carol gradually came to realize that merely dropping multimodal activities or active learning into classes is not new literacies instruction. When she developed lessons using a systematic approach to new literacies as the core of classroom teaching and learning, however, student engagement seemed to heighten, but—more importantly—so did the desire to find and communicate information about real questions that they raised about literacy and about their world. By January, when Carol was teaching students to interpret poems and communicate their interpretations in multimodal presentations created by PowerPoint software, technology seemed to play only a minor role in motivating the students' efforts on their projects. Carol and her students appeared to be viewing technology and multimodal work very differently from the way that Carol described it early in the school year as the "hook" with which to pull students in so that they would learn the "real" work of English 9.

Carol Adopts a New Literacies Stance

Throughout the fall semester and beyond, Carol gradually manifested in her teaching an understanding of the learning principles associated with new literacies. This development paralleled readings and discussions in her graduate class about multimodality (Kress, 2003), semiotic theory (Siegel, 2006), semiotic domains (Gee, 2003), situated and local knowledge (Barton & Hamilton, 2000; Street, 1994) and inquiry learning (Owens et al., 2002; Wells, 2001). As the semester progressed, she appeared to adopt a belief that gradual integration of all of these elements into her lessons would create the literacy learning in her classroom that she wanted to see. Carol was essentially taking on a new literacies stance. This means that as she learned about, discussed, and thought deeply about new literacies, Carol changed many of the usual ways that she conducted her English 9 classes.

Rather than the teacher-centered recitations (Tharp & Gallimore, 1988) that I often saw in much of September and early October, her new lessons were largely informed by ideas that the nature of learning is sociocultural (Rogoff, 1995; Vygotsky, 1978; Wells, 2001), constructivist (John-Steiner & Mahn, 1996; Vygotsky, 1978), semiotic (Kress, 2003), situated in the local knowledge and real inquiry of students (Street, 1994; Owens et al., 2002), and very often multimodal in nature (Gee, 2003; Kress, 2003). That Carol was recognizing the need to change the way that she was teaching literacy was reflected in a statement that she made in early November: "I've just changed my whole conception of what literacy is." By successfully adopting a new literacies stance and constructing a corresponding curriculum in her English 9 class, Carol gradually came to value the elements of new literacies less as a way to engage students and more as a way to do the real work of a literacy curriculum.

In the next sections, I will summarize the ways in which Carol's integration of new literacies into her English 9 class appeared to be generated by an increasingly clear understanding of new literacies theory. What can also be seen is that Carol's students increasingly seemed to regard the new literacies as avenues of self-discovery and self-expression when Carol built her curriculum around the following ideas.

Changing ideas about reading, writing, and the nature of texts: The box of clues. As Carol developed her new curriculum grounded in new literacies, she shifted her attention, and she also drew her students' attention, toward an expanded notion of texts and the common skills and strategies used to "read" and "write" them. In order to get this point across to students, she developed an interesting exercise that she now uses in the beginning of each new school year.

First, she asked students to help her to list the skills needed to be a good reader, focusing on various strategies, like making predictions, asking questions, visualizing, and connecting texts to other texts, self and world. As talk turned to these traditional channels, apparently signaled by words like "skills" and "strategies," students grew restless; some even assumed that glazed look that too often marks responses to reading instruction in our English classrooms. Students had apparently been there and done this before—that is, until Carol pulled out a box of objects familiar to students, though not always seen in an English classroom, that she called "clues." Carol's box included a popular teen magazine, a poem, a book, a music CD, a picture of a music video cover, and a video game. Students visibly changed their positions, sitting up and obviously attending to this unexpected, new development. Carol had their attention and used it to bring them back to her task of defining reading, by asking them to list five characteristics of their interaction with each of the five objects in her box. Students dictated their ideas like "remember happy or sad moments in our lives" from listening to music, "learn something useful" by reading a magazine, and "be entertained" by playing video games, and Carol wrote them on the whiteboard in the front of the room. Then she asked them to look at their comments and summarize any common features of the activities related to the objects in her box. Students easily saw the commonalities of interaction with the diverse literacy artifacts in Carol's box: We can learn from them, each can mean different things to different people, we can get information from them, and they can "show" emotion and tell a story. Most important, students volunteered, we need skills and strategies to understand them.

"Ah," Carol said, holding up the book, "so when we 'read' a book we are doing a lot of the same things that we are doing when we interact with all these other things. Does that mean that you can *read* a music video and you can *read* a video game?"

"No!" many immediately told her. It seemed that this was the first time that anyone had asked them to regard their own literacies—like music videos and games—as related in any way to what they did in school.

"But when we learn from this book or get information from it," Carol persisted as she pointed to the commonalities they had just listed on the board, "we are 'reading' aren't we? So why isn't it 'reading' when we do the same with a music video? We do make predictions when we read stories and when we play video games. We do visualize when we read books and also when we listen to music. We do make all kinds of connections all the time between what we are seeing and hearing and the events of our own lives."

This exercise using Carol's box of "clues" served at least two purposes: It helped students to connect the literacies that they used in their everyday lives to the school literacies that they often found dull and meaningless, or—at best—merely necessary for academic and social advancement. Making these new connections also seemed to make more transparent the idea that learning skills and strategies, like making predictions or synthesizing information, has real world applications that are relevant to their interests and can be useful for accomplishing their own purposes, not merely for completing school tasks imposed upon them; therefore, they now had a good reason for learning those skills and strategies.

By bringing "their" music and games into the classroom, Carol showed her students that she was working from the assumption that important knowledge takes many forms and resides in many places, not just in traditional, print-based texts (Barton & Hamilton, 2000; Sanchez, 2010). Thus, students could begin to see, perhaps for the first time, that popular culture has validity in school and that their local knowledge was an important resource for learning, ideas that would open many doors for their enthusiastic meaning making throughout the remainder of the school year in Carol's class. Examples of their subsequent responses are more fully described below as I illustrate specific moves that Carol made as she developed her new literacies stance.

Drawing on students' local knowledge and authentic inquiry: The song lyrics project. The song lyric project is a good example of how Carol drew upon her students' local knowledge about language to help them develop greater knowledge about academic language. During the class's study of poetry, one of the students mentioned to Carol that after some of their class discussions about poetic elements, he had begun to see many poetic devices and imagery in the songs that he often listened to. He asked if he could bring in one of his favorite songs and share it with the class as a poem.

Seeing an opportunity to continue the growing dialogue and collaborative knowledge-building that she was cultivating in her classes, Carol came up with a new project: The students would work in small groups, with each group choosing a favorite song, to develop a short lesson on poetic elements that they could teach the whole class. They would give Carol the song lyrics they were working with, and she would make copies for the whole class (a way to be sure that they were following her stricture about "appropriate" lyrics). She told them that each group would be able to play their song and then lead a class discussion based upon interesting ways in which they saw poetic elements used to create meaning. She also instructed them to think of "questions for the class to answer about the poem." "You're the teacher," Carol said the day before their presentations. "You're facilitating the whole thing, so be prepared."

When she told me about the new assignment, Carol explained that she thought that giving students an opportunity to use their local knowledge about music to learn about poetry might be valuable as a bridge between what the students enjoyed and what they needed to learn as the required ninth grade curriculum. In telling me about the new assignment, Carol had also connected it to the other new learning tasks that she had already created that year that were coming out of her growing understanding of new literacies:

> The assignments that I'm doing, it's really giving them [chances for] taking on more responsibility and making them think more critically than I've ever done before.... I think it's just all the extra [*she stops herself*]. No! I don't want to say "extra," the *new*, the *new* things that I'm doing. I'm really trying to put the new literacies in.... And I think also what a lot of teachers don't do, is I hold [students] accountable. Like, I have them find out information. Inquiry! They need to find out information and teach the class without me saying, "This is this" and "This is this." And I think that helps them also, being able to think more and not be afraid to really expand on their ideas in class.

Thus, Carol saw that the use of inquiry was actually a part of new literacies; in her mind, it seemed, the questions that her students would use for their inquiry would be extensions of the ways in which they used their local knowledge. Carol intended that her students' inquiry about their own music, combined with the dialogic activity of conducting a class discussion, would help them to construct knowledge about the ways that poets create poems and also about the ways that language is used to create personal meaning when readers read poems. And this is exactly what happened.

For two full days, the students conducted the class. Each group sat like a panel in the front of the room and talked about the questions that they had asked of the musical lyrics, and they asked their classmates to consider those questions with them. Carol had stipulated in her assignment that each student in the group had to contribute something to the class instruction, and so each person did say something, even those who were usually shy and reticent during other class discussions. Often, the students used some of the same kinds of questions that Carol had used when she had asked them to find poetic images in poems that she had brought to class.

Each group of students really was able to conduct a discussion without Carol's guidance—often for 5 to 10 minutes each. By this time, students had learned, from Carol's example and from her encouragement, how to create and maintain true dialogic interaction in the classroom. It was the students' local knowledge that drove these dialogic interactions. Because they were drawing from what they knew well and what interested them, students reached to make connections, not only to other kinds of music they had heard but with ideas that are important—perhaps even critical—for them to consider, like ideas about family coherence or avenues to personal and general well being. The students' local knowledge was the fertile context for their inquiry about poetic elements and for their dialogic meaning making.

When Carol and I later talked about the song lyric activity, she summarized the results of her somewhat spur-of-the-moment decision to give students the opportunity to apply the "insider principle," and she reflected upon the elements that came together to make the song lyric exercise such a powerful learning experience for her students:

> That was the best week! They taught for 40 minutes and I [initiated] absolutely nothing. And it carried the class! What I think has changed this year … with the students is that they are asking why. Or, they are giving reasons why. And I realized that when they were teaching the class, they instinctively asked the other kids, "Well, why did you think that?" What high schooler does that? I mean a kid gives an answer and they say to each other, okay, that's good.… Even though now they joke about it, they support their points, that's what they do. They say [Carol mimics them mimicking her], "Now, how are you going to support your answer with that?" But they are doing it. And it's never been there [in previous years' classes that she has taught].

It appeared that Carol's newfound understanding of the value of the students' local knowledge was also driving, to a large extent, her success in divesting herself of the role of "high, mighty, authority figure," as she put it. Consequently, when the students talked about the poetic elements in the songs that they themselves had selected and studied, they did so with confidence and were, more often than not, able to lead their peers in a discussion that was meaningful and interesting.

The important role of semiotics and multimodal complementarity: The Halloween stories. Probably the most salient changes in Carol's curriculum came about gradually as she introduced her students to the concepts related to multimodality and the way that modes work in complementary ways to create and expand meaning. From mid-October on, Carol's class engaged almost daily in multimodal activities. As they did, Carol often took the opportunity to teach explicitly how semiotic elements work in text to communicate and represent ideas. Speaking of the combination of visual and the verbal modes that has become increasingly common in today's textbooks and newspapers, Kress (1998) explains the complementary, interactive and important role each mode plays when these modal elements function together: "No, the two modes are not doing the same thing; and No, they are not merely coexisting; and Yes, there is, it seems, strong interaction between the two which could, over time, have real effects on language in the written mode" (p. 72). A similar point is made by Lemke (1998) who speaks of "joint meaning" that is produced as different modalities interact and intersect in multimodal texts: "Meanings in multimedia are not fixed and additive (the word meaning plus the picture meaning), but multiplicative (word meaning modified by image context, image meaning modified by textual context), *making a whole far greater than the simple sum of its parts*" (pp. 283–284, emphasis added).

Carol had learned in her graduate class about the principle of complementarity and about using a semiotic lens, and she simplified her newfound understandings about multimodality for her students. In late October, she started by introducing them to a writing lesson in which they inserted hyperlinks into a Word document as they wrote Halloween stories. By using the links, students were able to connect sounds and pictures into their stories, and Carol helped them to see how much more they could say and do using multimodal elements.

Students took advantage of new capabilities for adding multimodal story elements made possible by the computer. Pushed by the linguistic elements of their stories, some made drawings, using other computer software, or found pictures of disheveled, grotesque heads that were missing teeth to represent villains in their stories. Others found pictures of ramshackle houses that purportedly were the scenes of some very spooky goings on. Several varieties of shrieks, screams and creaking floors at intervals filled the computer lab where they worked.

One result of incorporating the multimodal resources that students found into their stories was a focus on more detailed and descriptive writing. Many soon caught on to the fact that in order to introduce the sound or visual effect made possible by the hyperlink, they had to write something descriptive that would signal the special effect. For example, doors didn't just open; they "creaked" open (Dani's paper). Characters laughed "maniacally" (Lucey's paper) and girls "stormed" upstairs (Amy's paper). Amy talked to me about how she and her classmates felt themselves prompted by the hyerlinks to reach for linguistic elements with which to color their stories. In fact, said Amy, she had found the assignment "harder" than more traditional creative writing assignments because of the challenge to use the hyperlinks in the story: "It gets people using more adjectives. They … add them in because they want the sound in there. So they're going to use more descriptive words." Thus, the technical tool was facilitating a cognitive response—thinking, searching and creating. At the same time, the multimodal elements in the story were driving students' linguistic development in much the way that their words had earlier driven their searches for multimodal resources.

Students used their cultural knowledge to add interesting and effective multimodal effects to "boost" the power of the words in their stories. In one of my favorite stories, "McDonald's Mayhem," Lucey wrote with black type on an orange background, traditional Halloween colors, and she used the story as a vehicle to write about a cultural icon, Ronald McDonald. In this story—which begins with two hyperlink cues, "scream sound" and "evil laugh effect"—Roy McDonald, evil twin of the famous Ronald, uses methods of mind control to attempt a takeover of McDonald's restaurants. Luckily, Ronald gets wind of the malfeasance in the nick of time, and after a knock-down, drag-'em-out fight, good is restored to the restaurant business. The amusing ending begins with the sound of a police siren and words, but it depends upon an amusing picture (see Figure 4.1) for its powerful climax that begins like this:

> **(Police car siren)** "I believe that is for you" said Alana with a snicker. Roy moaned.
>
> "Roy McDonald you are arrested for impersonating your brother and brainwashing the happy, overly peppy workers of McDonalds. Roy looked at Ronald. "I need to get a job at Burger King," said Roy to Ronald.
>
> "Let's go eat at McDonalds!" yelled Ronald. (Cheer sound effects)
>
> Many people do not believe this story but I do have proof, look at the picture below. SCROLL DOWN!!!

FIGURE 4.1 From "McDonald's Mahem" by Lucey

In response to an email I sent to Lucey asking her about her experience writing "McDonald's Mayhem," Lucey responded by telling me:

> The story ... was probably the best story I have written yet because of the sounds and being able to write about something I really am scared of—clowns! I learned that you can have a lot of fun writing a story. When you put sounds and music in, it is a lot easier to be creative and have fun. I never heard of inserting hyperlinks into a story. Actually, [now] I [have] started putting hyperlinks in my e-mails to my friends and family.

Many students expressed the same type of enthusiasm for the project, and this pleased Carol tremendously because she could tell that, like Lucey, other students were learning as well as having fun. "These are the most detailed stories I have ever received," she told me. Even more interesting, she told me on the morning of one of the days that the students were working on their stories that she had had a call earlier that day from the mother of one of the boys in her fifth period class. The mother had called to tell Carol what a difference she had seen in her son at home as a result of the Halloween story project. Her son, the mother told Carol, frequently struggled with school learning and was easily intimidated by school assignments, but during this particular week, he had told his mother enthusiastically about his story, had continued to work on it at home, and—in an uncharacteristic demonstration of confidence—had proudly shared it with his mother. The mother was so thrilled with her son's new-found enthusiasm for school that she had called to thank Carol for providing the means for this to happen.

After this experience, Carol took every opportunity to use multimodal texts in her lessons and to talk ever more explicitly about the elements of multimodal text. For example, when she was introducing study of the Paul Fleischman's (1998) novel, *Whirligig,* she first showed a music video with a similar theme to the novel and asked students to analyze and discuss the visual, musical, and linguistic elements of the video in order to understand that theme. Later, she and the students returned several times to their discussion of the music video's multimodal elements as they worked to analyze and understand the more esoteric novel.

The multimodal poetry project. The multimodal poetry interpretation project that Carol introduced in her curriculum warrants special attention because it is such an excellent example of how multimodal projects seemed to aid Carol's students' in learning their required English 9 curriculum, as well as lessons about the power of literacy. After learning about metaphors and similes and other poetic devices through analysis of both poems and song lyrics, Carol's students had an opportunity to select, prepare, and present an interpretation of a favorite poem (or one they themselves had written) using a multimodal format afforded by PowerPoint software. Carol continued to talk to students about multimodal elements as resources (Kress, 2003; New London Group, 1996). One day, for example, she talked to them about how colors, different sized fonts, and movement could be used in digital texts in ways similar to words and other print-centered graphics like punctuation and capital letters, teaching them to consider many semiotic elements as tools for information, representation, and communication. In discussions like this, she made thinking and talking about multimodality important to the students because they could see how much these elements contributed to what they wanted to say and how they were able to do so. She also engaged them in explicit discussion—and encouraged them to talk with each other while they were working on their poetry interpretations—about exactly how multimodal elements could help them to express their thoughts and ideas in very powerful ways. Some interesting conversations arose as a result. For example, a number of discussions started with questions like, "What color makes you think of … being alone?" or "What color is confusion?" or "Why do you have the black?" A notable interchange between Carol and Little Willy (all pseudonyms were student chosen) showing that he, like his classmates, was thinking about how color and shading can convey meaning:

Carol: [pointing to a figure on one of Little Willy's slides] Why did you darken his face?
Little Willy: Because he doesn't know who he is.

Little Willy appeared to be thinking semiotically; that is, he was intentionally using color to layer additional meaning onto the linguistic poem that he was interpreting. Even more notable was the fact that Little Willy, classified as eligible for special education services, was attending an "extra" English class, where he was receiving instruction in basic skills. His teacher there sometimes complained to Carol about his bad behavior and his inability to learn. This surprised both Carol and me since Little Willy participated fully in all of Carol's classes and turned in very acceptable assignments.

When I asked Little Willy one day about the difference in his two English classes, he couldn't tell me much about the work in his "extra" (remedial) English class except to say that the point of the reading there was "to [better] your fluency, and to ... better speech; I'm not sure." In speaking of Carol's class, however, he articulated what he saw as the benefit of the new literacies projects that he and his classmates often did: "When I do that stuff, I think about what's going on in the book. More than I would than just reading it." When I asked the point of reading books like *Whirligig,* he told me, "Um, to find, like, how to live." Little Willy's contrasting behaviors in his two English classes and his very different definitions of the "reading" he was doing in each class offer a good illustration of how much Carol's students seemed to regard her new literacies curriculum as meaningful and useful to them.

After listening to the students talk while they worked on their poetry interpretations and also after reading their written reflections about these projects, it was clear that Little Willy was not the only one who felt empowered by the multimodal tools that Carol put at their disposal. For example, Helena told me as she started to interpret "Conferring with Myself" by Emily Dickinson (1960, p. 66) that she was planning to relate Dickinson's poem to her own life. Therefore, she created on her title slide (Figure 4.2) a series of interlocking puzzle pieces as a metaphor for the many different pieces of her identity.

FIGURE 4.2 Helena's title slide

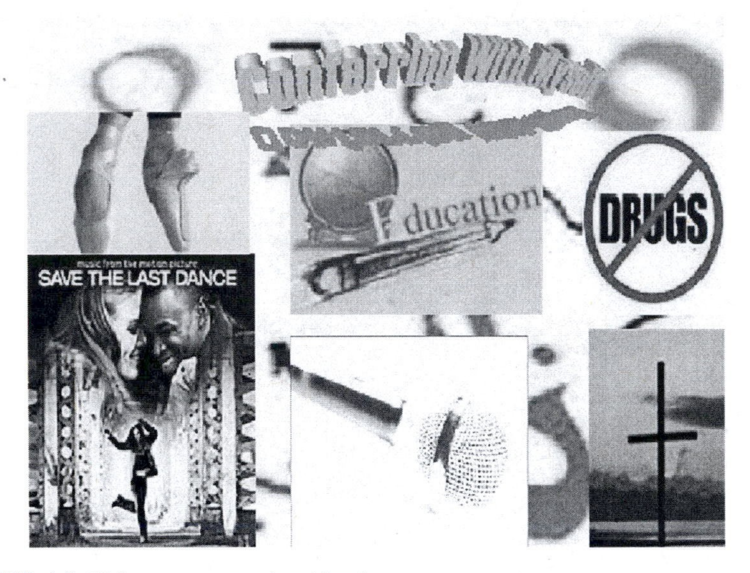

FIGURE 4.3 Helena represents her identity

Helena followed this slide with a second one (Figure 4.3) on which she placed various visual symbols to represent the beliefs—like her Christian faith and her renunciation of drugs—and the activities—like dancing and singing—that defined her. Interestingly, these pictures were layered on top of a series of colorful question marks that Helena used, she told me, to indicate her active search for a way to articulate exactly who she is. Thus, she was using image and symbol not only to reflect her identity, but also to show the process of figuring out what that identity was.

Like Helena, every one of Carol's other students used the power of multimodality to some degree to help them to represent the meanings that they had derived from the poems that they had chosen. In doing so, they demonstrated a growing ability to think semiotically and to convey meaning very skillfully using semiotic resources. Not only had they constructed meaning using visual and musical language, but they also recast or transmediated (Siegel, 2006) their ideas into academic language when they wrote assigned reflections about their process and about what they had learned from the entire project. In these reflections, two themes seemed to predominate. First, students declared in many different ways that they had learned a lot about poetry in general and about their chosen poem, specifically, from creating the poetry interpretation projects. For example, Sharla said, "I did see the poem different [sic] because the images make the poem make much more sense," and Monika wrote, "Once I put images to it and watched the slideshow myself it was almost like the meaning was written out in big bold letters."

A second theme that appeared to run through the students' written reflections was related to their use of multimodality. As can be seen by their statements above, many expressed a growing awareness that rich meaning can be made with other modal elements besides the linguistic and that using multimodal elements can deepen and augment meaning created by words. Many students, for instance wrote some variation of what Ralphy said, "Using pictures, music, and movement of images helped to interpret what the message of the poem is."

Conclusion

The National Commission on Teaching and America's Future (1996) claims that "no other intervention can make the difference that a knowledgeable, skillful teacher can make in the learning process" (cited in Allington & Johnston, 2000, p. 1). As I traced Carol's learning about new literacies and how she gradually implemented what she was learning into her English 9 classroom, I was struck by the aptness of these words. Through conscientious study and reflection about the theoretical basis of new literacies, Carol assumed a new literacies stance that was both sociocultural—drawing on elements such as dialogism, inquiry-based learning, and students' local knowledge (Gee, 2003; Wells, 2001)—and semiotic—drawing on elements of multimodality and semiotic grammars (Kress, 1998, 2003; Unsworth, 2001).

The more she saw her students participate and learn the required curricular knowledge of English 9 from the activities she designed and redesigned (New London Group, 1996; Walsh, 2009), the more she realized that new literacies shouldn't be used as a "hook" to pull students into learning or even as "a spoonful of sugar" (Kist, 2005) to make learning more palatable. Instead, when new literacies were the daily work of the class, students learned literary elements, poetic devices, and rhetorical methods. They also used reading and writing strategies in ways that previous classes never had before. Rather than give her students traditional quizzes or artificial writing assignments to test their knowledge—as she did in September and was sorely disappointed at the results—Carol used rubrics and other authentic assessment tools for analysis of their multimodal constructions as well as their discussions, to determine if they were learning the material of the course, but also to assess if they were consistently using new literacies in their discussions, their projects, and their writing.

For their part, the students seemed to learn better the mandated curriculum, a point often confirmed in my discussions with Carol during our frequent talks. When I talked to Carol at the end of the school year, moreover, she told me that students' scores on the end-of-the year district English 9 exam were, overall, the best that she had ever seen from her classes. She was thrilled and determined to continue to build her new literacies curriculum.

On a simple questionnaire that Carol allowed me to ask students to complete on the last day that I observed in their class in early February, I asked if they had changed in any way, especially in regard to how they understood or felt about reading and writing. Every student wrote about some kind of personal growth or new understanding of literacy processes. Many strongly indicated that they saw themselves as real readers and writers and important members of a learning community. For example, Max wrote, "Now we have seen so many different ways to understand reading. This class has opened up my eyes." Monika expressed feelings similar to those of many of her classmates when she said, "I learned that sometimes reading can be fun." She also added, "I learned more about interpreting poems, and my already strong feeling for writing poems and stories increased." Helena said that she had learned that "writing is basically words written into paragraphs that represent your life." Brian, who was often quiet in class, wrote, "I've changed. I'm not afraid to talk in class anymore." And Little Willy said, "[In] eighth grade I really didn't understand English. I really didn't pay attention. Now I pay attention and try to figure out stuff."

In discussing video games and projective identities, Gee (2004) says, "If learners in classrooms carry learning so far as to take on a projective identity, something magic happens.... The learner comes to know that he or she has the capacity, at some level, to take on the virtual identity as a real world identity" (p. 302). The statements of Carol's students—those quoted here as well as told to me directly, written in reflections they gave to Carol, or said to each other while working together on projects—strongly suggest that some of the "magic" that Gee mentions was at play in Carol's classroom. The new literacies projects that her students so enthusiastically embraced provided them with many opportunities to take on projective identities as readers and writers that became their real world selves.

Implications

These examples taken from Carol's new literacies classroom have strong implications for teacher education. If we are to train our teachers to be as successful as Carol was in teaching important literacy skills to their students, we teacher educators must help them to shape an epistemological perspective that is consistent with a strong new literacies stance. That is, teachers must come to understand that literacy is social and cultural practice shaped by multiple sign systems, and that students must have opportunities to use their situated, local knowledge, as well as dialogue and inquiry, in order to transform their participation and activity into learning and identity building. The many examples of the literacy practices and the literacy learning of Carol's students are persuasive evidence that such secondary English instruction is effective. Teachers seeking the same kind of successful learning in their classrooms must develop a deep understanding of the theory and learning principles that will generate and support their own new literacies stance.

References

Allington, R. L., & Johnston, Peter H. (2000). *What do we know about effective fourth-grade teachers and their classrooms?* (No. 13010). Albany, NY: The National Research Center on English Learning & Achievement.

Alvermann, D. E. (2002). Effective literacy instruction for adolescents. *Journal of Literacy Research, 34*, 189–208.

Bailey, N. M. (2006). Designing social futures: Adolescent literacy in and for New Times. Unpublished doctoral dissertation. Buffalo, NY: University at Buffalo, SUNY.

Barton, D., & Hamilton, M. (2000). Literacy practices. In D. Barton, M. Hamilton, & R. Ivanic (Eds.), *Situated literacies: Reading and writing in context* (pp. 7–15). New York: Routledge.

Bean, T. W., Bean, S. K., & Bean, K. F. (1999). Intergenerational conversations and two adolescents' multiple literacies: Implications for redefining content area literacy. *Journal of Adolescent & Adult Literacy, 42*, 438–448.

Bruce, B. C. (1997). Literacy technologies: What stance should we take? *Journal of Literacy Research, 29*, 289–309.

Chandler-Olcott, K., & Mahar, D. (2003). Adolescents' *anime*-inspired "fanfictions": An exploration of Multiliteracies. *Journal of Adolescent & Adult Literacy, 46*, 556–566.

Cohen, B., & Meyer, R. (2004). The Zine project: Writing with a personal perspective. *Language Arts, 82*(2), 129–138.

Dickinson, E. (1960). Conferring with myself. In T. H. Johnson (Ed.), *Complete Poems* (p. 66). Boston: Little Brown.

Fleischman, P. (1998). *Whirligig.* New York: Dell Laurel-Leaf.

Gee, J. P. (2003). *What video games have to teach us about learning and literacy.* New York: Palgrave Macmillan.

Gee, J. P. (2004). New times and New Literacies: Themes for a changing world. In A. F. Ball & S. W. Freedman (Eds.), *Bakhtinian perspectives on language, literacy, and learning* (pp. 279–306). Cambridge, UK: Cambridge University Press.

Hull, G. A., & Schultz, K. (Eds.). (2002). *School's out: Bridging out-of-school literacies with classroom practice.* New York: Teachers' College Press.

John-Steiner, V., & Mahn, H. (1996). Sociocultural approaches to learning and development: A Vygotskian framework. *Educational Psychologist, 31*(3/4), 191–206.

Kadjer, S., Frey, N., & Fink, L. (2006). Meeting readers: Using visual literacy narratives in the classroom. *Voices From the Middle, 14*(1), 13–19.

Kalantzis, M. & Cope, B. (2008). *New Learning: Elements of a science of education*. Cambridge, UK: Cambridge University Press.

Kist, W. (2005). *New literacies in action: Teaching and learning in multiple media.* New York: Teachers College Press.

Kress, G. (1998). Visual and verbal modes of representation in electronically mediated communication: The potentials of new forms of text. In I. Snyder (Ed.), *Page to screen: Taking literacy into the electronic era* (pp. 53–79). London: Routledge.

Kress, G. (2003). *Literacy in the new media age.* New York: Routledge.

Labbo, L. D. (2004). From writing workshop to multimedia workshop. *Language Arts, 82*(2), 119.

Lankshear, C., & Knobel, M. (2007). Sampling "the New" in new literacies. *A New Literacies Sampler.* New York: Peter Lang.

Lemke, J. L. (1998). Metamedia literacy: Transforming meanings and media. In D. Reinking, M.C. McKenna, L. D. Labbo, & R. D. Kieffer (Eds.), *Handbook of literacy and technology: Transformations in a post-typographic world* (pp. 283–301). Mahwah, NJ: Erlbaum.

Lewis, C., & Chandler-Olcott, K. (2008). From screen to page: Secondary English teachers' perspectives on redesigning their teaching of literature in a new literacies era. In K. M. Leander & D. W. Rowe, K. Dickinson, M. K. Hundley, R. T. Jimenez, & V. J. Risko (Eds.), *58*th *Yearbook of the National Reading Conference* (pp. 205–217). Oak Creek, WI: National Reading Conference, Inc.

Lewis, C. & Fabos, B. (2005). Instant messaging, literacies, and social identities. *Reading Research Quarterly, 40,* 470–501.

McVee, M. B., Bailey, N. M., & Shanahan, L.E. (2008). Technology lite: Advice and reflections for the technologically unsavvy. *Journal of Adolescent & Adult Literacy, 51,* 444–448.

Miller, S., & Borowitz, S. (2006). *Why multimodal literacies*? Buffalo, NY: SUNY Press/University at Buffalo GSE Publications.

The New London Group. (1996). A pedagogy of multiliteracies: Designing social futures. *Harvard Educational Review, 66*(1), 60–92.

O'Brien, D. G., & Bauer, E. B. (2005). New literacies and the institution of old learning. *Reading Research Quarterly, 40,* 120–131.

Owens, R. F., Hester, J. L., & Teale, W. H. (2002). Where do you want to go today? Inquiry-based learning and technology integration. *The Reading Teacher, 55,* 616–625.

Prensky, M. (2001). Digital natives, digital immigrants. Part 1. *On the Horizon, 9*(5), 1–6.

Rogoff, B. (1995). Observing sociocultural activity on three planes: Participatory appropriation, guided participation, and apprenticeship. In J. V. Wertsch, P. DelRio, & Amelia Alvarez (Eds.), *Sociocultural studies of mind* (pp. 139–164). Cambridge, UK: Cambridge University Press.

Sanchez, D.M. (2010). Hip-hop and a hybrid text in a postsecondary English class. *Journal of Adolescent & Adult Literacy, 53*(6), 478–487.

Seglem, R., & Witte, S. (2009). You gotta see it to believe it: Teaching visual literacy in the English classroom. *Journal of Adolescent & Adult Literacy, 53,* 216–226.

Siegel, M. (2006). Rereading the signs: Multimodal transformations in the field of Literacy Education. *Language Arts, 84*(1), 65–77.

Street, B. (1994). What is meant by local literacies? *Language and Education, 8*(1-2), 9–17.

Tharp, R., & Gallimore, R. (1988). *Rousing minds to life.* New York: Cambridge University Press.

Unsworth, L. (2001). *Teaching multiliteracies across the curriculum: changing contexts of text and image in classroom practice.* Philadelphia: Open University Press.

Vygotsky, L. S. (1978). *Mind in society: The development of higher psychological processes.* Cambridge, MA: Harvard University Press.

Walsh, C. S. (2009). The multi-modal redesign of school texts. *Journal of Research in Reading, 32*(1), 126–136.

Wells, G. (2001). The case for dialogic inquiry. In G. Wells (Ed.), *Action, talk, and text: Learning and teaching through inquiry* (pp. 171–194). New York: Teachers College Press.

5

"BEING GREAT FOR SOMETHING"

Composing Music Videos in a High School English Class

James Cercone

It's a cold morning in late November and loud rock music is playing from two large, vintage speakers in Joel Malley's 12th-grade English course, "Mass Media and Video Productions." Under a swirl of guitars, heavy drums, and bass the lead female singer of The Veronicas wails out the lyrics of "Revolution," a song of personal empowerment, full of youthful energy.

Students' heads bop and sway to the beat, originating from a student's iPod that is plugged into an old stereo; some sing along quietly to themselves, others literally dance in their seats. As the music fades, Joel (Mr. Malley to his students) turns to the student who has chosen to play this song for class and says: "Mercy, the floor is yours." With that, the student begins reading from a journal she composed the night before. "I picked this song just because it says 'I am a revolution.' I think that I would like to be great for something, I don't care what, just something ..." She's interrupted by a few hoots and hollers of encouragement. As they subside she continues, "I'm really excited because I know exactly what I'm going to do for this video ..."

Walking by and looking in, it might be hard for some to identify this as an English Language Arts classroom. Students were not reading from textbooks or writing five paragraph essays. Nor was the teacher discussing the symbolic relevance of a particular scene in a novel, or the function of a literary element, or the intention of any given author. There were no worksheets or other familiar totems of a traditional classroom space. Instead, students' iPods were plugged in and loud rock music permeated the room. What, exactly, was going on here?

The Problem

Due to dramatic changes in literacy as we have known it, English teachers face a difficult challenge. English Language Arts classrooms—often sites of sterile literary preservation, plot summary and the five-paragraph essay—must change, too. We are all surrounded by new ways of making meaning, new ways of working in the world. Young people, in particular, are engaged with the world in drastically different ways from the generations that preceded them. Their access to information and modes of communication are unprecedented in human history. They learn, communicate, and create in strikingly different ways. They engage socially over a wide variety of media, have unparalleled access to changing ways of communicating with one another, of obtaining news and information and seeking out entertainment. Of course, these changes are not limited to young people. All of our professional, social ,and civic lives have been impacted by technological changes. We video chat with loved ones half a world away, conduct important business meetings from the comfort of our homes, and catch up on work-related email on our phones while on vacation. Our ways of connecting with and talking back to the world are varied, multiple, and digital. Yet, despite these sweeping changes many English Language Arts classrooms look strikingly similar to the classrooms of previous centuries, operating under what Lankshear and Bigum (1999, p. 455) refer to as "business as usual," employing instructional practices that direct attention towards rote memorization, summative assessments and disembodied learning.

A New Kind of Learning

Even if we are interested in moving away from traditional instructional practices and incorporating popular culture and digital technologies into our classrooms, doing so effectively is difficult. All around us are models of the old way of doing things. We need new models—classrooms where teachers have taken up these new technologies, classrooms where students engage with popular media and digital technologies in order to make meaning. This chapter provides an opportunity to step inside one of these classrooms, a media- and technology-rich 11th- and 12th-grade English Language Arts course taught by Joel Malley at Apple Central High School, a diverse first-ring, working-class suburb of a medium-sized, high-poverty city in the Northeast. Drawing on my year of observation in this class, in this chapter I examine the work students and their teacher undertook as they worked through a music video composing project. I provide classroom examples of the literacy practices members of this class engaged in, sharing student writing and video projects along the way. I then conclude with suggestions on how ELA and other content area teachers might incorporate some of these activities in their own classrooms.

While this chapter focuses on the practical dimensions of using digital video composing in the ELA classroom, it is helpful to take note of what research has taught us about the use of digital video composing as an instructional tool. Several studies have pointed towards the agentive effects of digital video composing in out-of-school settings (Hull, 2003; Hull & Nelson, 2005) and the learning opportunities they present when used within classrooms (Bailey, 2009; Borowicz, 2005; Bruce, 2009; Cercone, 2010; Costello, 2010; Miller, 2007, 2008, 2010; Ranker, 2008a, 2008b). What we can glean from these studies for the purposes of this chapter is that digital video composing provides students with an opportunity to engage in meaning making using multiple modes, including image, print and sound—the different "texts" that make up a digital video. When combining these texts in their video, students must be aware of how these different modes speak to one another and whether they are working together to communicate the students' ideas. This is often active and collaborative work, with students up and about, filming and acting in each other's productions. This learning is powerful and participatory (Jenkins, Purushotma, Weigel, Clinton, & Robison, 2007), engaging students to work with multiple forms of media, and with one another, to make meaning.

A New Kind of Classroom

The diverse students of this class gathered in a small room. Their teacher was new to the school during this study, though he had 5 years of prior experience teaching in a large urban school district. Mercy, Destiny, and Mark, the focal students of the larger study this chapter is drawn from, were all seniors at the school and were taking the course to complete their required year of senior English. The focal students reflected the diversity of the student body, in the work they undertook, as well as in their racial and ethnic background. Mercy, a Latina student whose work will be featured in this chapter, created a music video that expressed her developing philosophy about life. Mercy described her previous experiences in English, commenting that her teacher

> would give us a packet of questions, like, 10 questions for each chapter, kind of thing, and after you read the chapter—or while you read the chapter, you answer the questions. And me and my friends would, like, assign chapters to each other. We'd read through them throughout the entire period and then answer them while we were reading and then, like, switch papers and turn them in.

Destiny, an African American student, created a video that she hoped delivered a message about gender and self respect to her peers. Destiny's experiences in some of her English classes at the school were similar to Mercy's. She explained that her previous year of English was "boring" and she would simply be asked to "listen to the lectures, take a test or write a paper." Mark, a Caucasian student, created a music video that sought to capture the fleeting moments of life he felt were so important. Mark described his work in class underscoring many of the themes other students pointed out, remarking that one English teacher would "give us notes, which are just notes with blanks in it, and you gotta' fill in the blanks with whatever he's teaching ... all you really need is notes and a worksheet."

Setting the Stage with Writing and Discussion

Students in the class engaged in a variety of writing assignments, often personal in nature. They shared that writing in class, discussing it with one another and providing feedback. Joel then asked students to use that writing to create a digital video project. These projects were on a variety of topics, from music videos, and video projects inspired by National Public Radio's "This I Believe" series, to mini-documentaries and public service announcements. Each project was between 2 and 5 minutes. In this true 21st-century classroom, students used digital video cameras provided by the school to film their videos and then edited the raw footage using Apple's iMovie software. Joel also used ning.com, an online social space, for the course. On this site students posted their writing and homework responses, shared their videos and commented on one another's work. Joel also provided all his students with email addresses using the school-safe, free email service provided by gaggle.net. All final videos were screened in class and uploaded to the course website for viewing.

A community of writers. In preparation for the music video, students read and discussed an essay by the author Nick Hornsby, which linked the song "Puff the Magic Dragon" to the author's memories of his son. Joel then frontloaded (Wilhelm, Hackett, & Baker, 2002) the music video project by asking students to write a journal about a song they found meaningful to them. Frontloading, Wilhelm argues, "helps the students use what they already know (the "near to home"), so that they can build on this to move "further from home," learning new concepts and strategies" (p. 45). The initial assignment Joel developed set the stage for the work students would be undertaking by situating the writing assignment in terms of their own experiences. He tapped into students' familiarity and personal connections with popular culture by asking them to pick a song that was personally important and meaningful and to write a journal discussing why.

Students composed this journal as a homework assignment. Joel then asked students to share and discuss this writing in class. In these cases, students' journals were personal, but varied in topic and tone. Unlike Mercy, whose writing about The Veronicas' song "Revolution" was focused on personal empowerment, Destiny shared her journal about the song "I Love My Life" by Noriega, striking a decidedly nostalgic and reflective tone. She read, "This song reminds me when I was little and me and my older sister would listen to that song over and over again and we would just zone out and think about our lives ... I thought about my life a lot while I listened to this song and thought about what my life consisted of and who I am and where I came from." Students listened attentively as she continued, saying that she had decided, however, to make her movie about "That Thing" by Lauryn Hill. "This song is about the differences between boys and girls and what boys want and what girls want. I first heard this song at my eighth-grade birthday party. I like Lauryn Hill as a female artist because she speaks the truth and doesn't talk about what other girls talk about."

Mark, chose to write about the song "Over The Rainbow/What A Wonderful World" by Israel Kamakawiwo Ole', a Hawaiian medley of the two American popular music standards. Mark read his response to the class:

> Music is very important to me ... There are so many things within each song that holds me to it ... things that hold true to many aspects of my life. One song in particular holds many emotions behind it, emotions that connect to memories and thoughts of great importance. The song is "Over the Rainbow" by Israel Kamakawiwo Ole'. On some days it's a sad song, and other days it's very happy, but whatever the day is it is always enjoyable.... The lyrics and melody are different than the normal version, making the song familiar but new—sort of like a dream of a place you never were when you were young but ended up going there later in life. I can only hope that my videos will convey these feelings and emotions to my audience ...

After Mark finished reading, Joel turned to the class and asked for comments. One student remarked, "I liked how he described how it had a certain mood to it." Joel responded, "Yeah, I wrote that down too, 'some days sad, some days happy' what do you mean?" After a brief discussion that included the various TV shows and films the song had appeared in, Joel attempted to direct Mark's thinking towards the video he would make. How might he capture the ideas in his journal on film? I would find Joel asking this question often of Mark and other students throughout the year. How might they take their writing and develop it into a film?

The initial writing opportunity provided by Joel's journal assignment afforded students the chance to connect personally with the project, but it also served as an opportunity to jump-start their thinking about the movie they would be making. In this case, the writing Joel asked his students to engage in prior to starting the video project was generative and contextual—it was writing for a purpose. By asking Mark to consider how he would capture his thoughts on film, Joel asked him to begin a metacognitive, reflective process—and to begin thinking like a filmmaker. Indeed, all students engaged in this form of higher order thinking as they considered ways they might match visual elements in their videos to the larger ideas, themes and issues that sprang from their journals. Though they were engaged in video composing, students in

Joel's class talked with one another about their writing and its implications for their projects on a regular basis.

Joel shares his journal. Joel, too, entered this community. After a few other students read their journals and discussed the initial ideas they had for their music videos, Joel handed out copies of a long piece of writing he had done about a song that was important to him, "Naked As We Came," by Iron and Wine, a soft, folk-infused meditation on love, life, and death. As the song played, Joel read his journal to class:

> This album was the soundtrack for the early days of my son's existence on this earth … Each morning I would wake and put on this CD first as I rocked and soothed and fed my son. I'd put coffee on and sway back and forth as dawn peered into my skylight. Nobody else and nothing else seemed to exist …

His piece concluded with a meditation on fatherhood, of the important role he needed to play in his son's life. He finished to a round of applause from his students, thanked them for "indulging him," and asked if there are any "lingering questions."

Joel then described what he would do next if he were going to develop this piece of writing into a video. "My next step would be to take what I wrote and kind of figure out what would be my voice-over." Ending class, Joel informed his students of the agenda for the rest of the week, telling them that they were going to watch some music videos to see how professional directors constructed them and that they would begin planning and creating their videos. These shared stories were a regular, and essential, feature of the class throughout the year. The initial work for the project, the purposeful writing and discussing, the sharing of these stories set the stage for the work students engaged in as they worked with their writing, popular media and technology to develop their videos.

Introducing the Music Video Project

Joel's official introduction to the music video project helps to illustrate the various roles he played as the teacher of the course and the workshop approach he took to instruction. The introduction, coming a few days after students read their journals in class, serves as an example of a typical day in the class and helps to show Joel's approach to teaching this course.

Students shuffled in slowly the next day. "Did you grade my stuff?" a student asked, rummaging through a plastic box, looking for his journal from the previous day. Another student almost wandered into the room accidentally, her face focused on the screen of her phone. Sitting near the back of the room Mark, dressed from head to toe in black, told Mercy, fashionably dressed in a hooded sweatshirt, tube socks, sneakers, and a jean skirt, "I didn't do any of my work in any of my classes." Next to Mark a group of girls chatted and laughed with one another as they took their seats.

With class about to start, students seated at the computer tables turned their chairs towards the center of the room, still talking with one another. The bell rang, two boys sleepily stepped into the room, and Joel began handing out an assignment sheet for the music video project.

After addressing a few individual questions, he began reading from the handout."Your task is to create a conceptual narrative …" Joel moved around the room energetically as he explained the assignment. Students watched him, listening to his overview. Stepping gingerly between them, in the small room where students were clustered together sitting at small tables and in computer chairs, he emphasized the importance of using visual metaphors in the project. "Don't just say something, suggest it as well," he entreated them. He explained that they would develop a voice-over narrative from their journals. They would record this narrative and use it in their films. Students listened, still chatting among themselves. He announced the due date, Wednesday December 17, encouraging them to stay focused during the project, commenting, "Remember how long editing takes." He asked if there were any questions; there were none, and he concluded the introduction with an enthusiastic, "Let's go!"

In a split second there was a flurry of activity. Some students sat and talked with one another about their projects, while others listened to music on iPods, or their computers, still trying to decide what songs to pick. Some students grabbed the storyboard templates Joel had placed on one of the round tables and began planning out shots for their videos. Joel had not identified this as a requirement for the project, stating only that students could use them to "generally plan-out" their ideas for their videos.

The Daily Practices of the Digital Video Workshop

Making the rounds. For the rest of the period Joel Malley was in motion—moving from student to student, talking with them about their projects, reading over their writing, answering their questions, and providing assistance with technological problems that arose—a process I would witness many times during my observations. From time to time he would make an announcement to the class, something triggered by the conversation he was having with an individual student at the moment, "Just a quick thing I meant to mention," he projected to the class, "use the storyboard for … don't feel like you have to do a frame by frame …" In another instance he noticed one student had searched the Internet for the lyrics of the song she was thinking of using and he commented to the class, "what I've seen a couple of people do, which I think is a really good idea, is to bring up the lyrics." In such cases he raised his voice-over the rumble of students at work in the room. This method of moving through the classroom while sharing student practices with the class is particularly useful in understanding the effectiveness of Joel's teaching, his classroom, and the learning his students engaged in throughout the year. It further illustrated the workplace-like atmosphere of the room. By touching base with students and being aware of the work they were engaged in, Joel was able to share their practices with the class. He was able to provide instructional support at the point of each student's need, a clear example of differentiated instruction in practice. As Joel moved purposefully around the room, making a path along the "U" of the computer tables, he engaged students in focused discussions about their ideas, their plans, and the work at hand.

Laughter and energy permeated the space as students talked with one another, music playing from their computers. As the music grew louder, Joel would often refer students to headphones they could use. Mark, after a short comment to a student across the room about the lack of alternative artists represented in the American Music awards show the previous night, asked if there was a transition of glass shattering he could use in his film. Mercy discussed another student's video, suggesting shots to her peer and asking questions about the song she was using, while Joel chatted briefly with another student about where she might place her voice-over in her film.

Supporting with talk. These conversations, from the casual talk surrounding their lives and more pointed discussions about their work in class, were often ambient, creating a coffee shop atmosphere in the classroom. These conversations became social hotspots for learning. Joel's way of working with students allowed him to talk directly with them about the videos they were working on, offering constructive comments throughout the compositional process. After watching some of the footage Mercy had put together for her video *I am a Revolution*, he provided immediate feedback, commenting. "I love the shots, lots of good shots ... Don't cut off peoples' heads. I loved the idea; it's a cool concept and fits with the song." Referring to some of the video Mercy had captured of students in the hallways between classes, he commented that he liked the images of "human beings" going about their lives and their "personalities" in her film ... "just try and make it look composed, consider where the person is in the shot .... but I'd say 8 out of 10 shots pop." In this, and countless other instances, Joel engaged students in these social hotspots to support their learning, entering into their zones of proximal development (Vygotsky, 1978) to provide direct assistance at the point of each student's need.

Discussing rough drafts. Over the ensuing weeks, Joel and his students worked on developing their videos. Students filmed in and out of class, edited their movies, and assisted each other along the way. A true collaborative atmosphere filled the room as Joel cycled around, talking with his students about their work. With a little over a week before their winter vacation, Joel asked students to write a journal detailing their work on the video, calling it a "Rant, Rave and Reflect" opportunity.

> If I could, ah … if you are facing your computer and touching a keyboard if you could hot potato that and turn around, like physically turn your desk or your chair around … so as your executive producer I want to gauge how far along you guys are, and also I want to see if there are any challenges that are consistently running through any of your projects, see if we can trouble shoot and talk about them.

Before students began writing he reminded them that they had the rest of the week and the following Monday to work on this project, but that it needed to be finished before students left for winter vacation. After giving students several minutes to write their journal, he asked if any one wanted to share their thoughts. After one eager student shared a part of his video he was especially proud of, Joel quickly turned back to the class, asking if anyone else had a shot they wanted to share. Mark jumped in explaining that he had a shot of the sun hitting the clouds, commenting that "it's the first thing you see when the video opens." Joel asked, "How does it fit into the story" and Mark responded, "the main part of the whole story is that, um … no matter how difficult or how tough your life can get, there's always things and people that make it worthwhile, worth living … memorable about it, so that's what I'm trying to do is catch those moments." Destiny also volunteered, and, after playing the video, the class discussed her approach to filming the shot, a scene of her running down the hallway.

Another student volunteered and explained that the video she was making about her grandfather was "too sad to make" and that she didn't know how to match up the shots with what the song was saying, referencing lines like "I miss you" and "I'm so sad you slipped away," particularly because her grandfather was no longer alive for her to film. Mark offered some advice: "You really don't need a person to describe that per se, like any kind of picture or item or inanimate object fit in with the right kind of shot and music tone can set that feeling in. So, like, you don't necessarily have a person crying to instill that feeling into a person watching." Joel referred the class back to a music video for the song "Cut" by Johnny Cash they had watched, explaining how the director used a variety of images to convey the feelings of the song. He then reframed Mark's comments into a simpler statement, "I think what Mark was saying is that you can say things without saying them." He asked the student if these comments helped at all, she responded that it "sort of does," to which Joel commented, "Well, let's get together and talk it through." With that he apologized to the class for "taking up a work day with talk" and informed students that he would be happy to tack another day on to the project if they felt that stealing the day for discussion "had been too much of a hindrance."

It is important to note that Joel did provide additional time after students returned from winter recess, allowing them to work on their projects their first week back to school. This additional time was important, as students needed the technology available in the classroom to edit their movies and the social space to support one another in their work.

Making Learning Public: Music Video Screenings

The culmination of the music video project was a screening of student videos before a weeklong break in classes for January examinations. During this time, Joel acted as a Master of Ceremonies, introducing students, their videos, and facilitating short discussions around each film. The screenings took three class periods. For each screening day Joel provided popcorn, chips, drinks, and other snacks. There was an electric atmosphere in the room during the screenings: students were bright-eyed and noticeably excited to view each other's completed films. Joel asked for students to volunteer their films for screening, an opportunity many were eager to sign up for. At this time a few students were still coming in to Joel's classroom during free periods, lunches, even after school, to finish their music videos, an opportunity he always extended to his students.

Mercy: "I am a Revolution." On the first day of screenings Joel commented, "You have made some wonderful films … You are the directors of these videos, this is an opportunity for you to hear from your peers." Mercy volunteered to go first, introducing her video for "Revolution" by The Veronicas as "pretty self-explanatory." Played from Joel's computer and projected onto a large screen that descended from the ceiling over a wall of the classroom, the video energized students as they once again tapped their feet to the music and danced in their seats, this time laughing and pointing out friends who appeared in the film. Mercy opened the video with an over the shoulder shot of a young person writing what appeared to be a journal entry. She explained that this shot came from another student in the class who was going to use it in her video but had decided not to. As the young person in the video wrote, Mercy began her voice-over,

> The life you lead is an amazing thing, live every moment and always do you. No matter what you do someone somewhere will recognize your accomplishment and appreciate what you have donated to our world. So never hold back and never let go of your dreams. Because anything and everything you do is great. Never let anyone tell you what will make you happy. And be not what looks cool. Be weird, mad, intense, sweet, smart. Be your own you. Day and night.

Mercy explained that the last lines of the voice-over came from a poster she had made by cutting out words from a magazine and pasting them together to form a poem. She hung the poster on her wall at home. Mercy explained that the poster was a good fit for the video, "Because my video is pretty much, 'Be Yourself'." As the voice-over finished the music began and Mercy switched to a series of shots that featured students and teachers in the school who completed the phrase "I am ______," filling in the blank with a phrase they felt best captured their personality at that time. They then held up these signs to the camera. Joel, featured in the film, filled in the front of his sign with, "I am learning. Constantly." On the back of the paper, which is also featured in the video, he wrote "all sorts of things." He held the sign over his laptop with one hand, while he typed on the keyboard with the other.

Students in the class took up Mercy's request in creative ways as well. Mercy featured several of the students in one shot standing in the middle of the hallway, holding their signs. Mercy arranged the students so that each sign was visible. They were posed as if ready to take a group portrait. As the video played students walked toward the camera holding up their signs. Mark, who is featured in this sequence, had written, "I am truth in its purist (sic) form" (Figure 5.1).

Other students delivered bombastic messages; Ted's read, "I am Beast," while another student wrote, "I am the Greatest." Mercy placed the video clips of students walking through the hallways between these shots, in effect, breaking up the long group sequence, something Joel had suggested Mercy consider. She revisited this type of editing later in the video, this time taking the filming outside. In this sequence snow flurries fluttered across the video as five female students from the class walked out the front doors of the school holding their

FIGURE 5.1 Mark presenting his "I Am" sign in Mercy's video.

FIGURE 5.2 Students displaying their "I Am" signs in front of the school in Mercy's video.

signs. Mercy filmed each student as they walked individually out of the school doors. As they walked toward the camera, they stopped and Mercy focused her camera on the sign they were holding so the viewer might read it. When one student had been filmed, another exited from the door, walked toward the camera and took their place next to and slightly behind the student who had preceded them (Figure 5.2). Mercy explained this shot as representing "togetherness even though we are, like, all different."

Again, Mercy inserted other video clips to break up this sequence. One of these video clips was of her performing a cartwheel in a school hallway. She explained this shot as "a little of my own visual metaphor … that if you try hard enough you can do amazing things, that takes practice." She finished the video by throwing all the signs over a stairwell railing from the second floor of the school. This sequence was filmed in two takes. The first take featured Mercy tossing the signs over the railing. The camera was situated below Mercy as she threw the signs over (Figure 5.3). From this angle the signs floated down across the screen.

Mercy then switched the shot. She again threw the signs over, but chose to film them straight on as they fell. The final shot of the sequence, a close up of the signs, was filmed from above, as they lay scattered on the stairs.

After Mercy's video finished playing, students briefly commented about specific points in the film they liked. One student commented that she liked a clip that Mercy had added—a backwards effect—to the shot of Mercy doing a cartwheel in the hallway set in reverse motion. Mark liked the ending of the film, commenting that it "brought everything to a sort of conclusion," with Destiny adding that she enjoyed the diversity of the people Mercy had included.

The video screening took three class periods and offered students an opportunity to share their work, something they found meaningful. Mark noted it

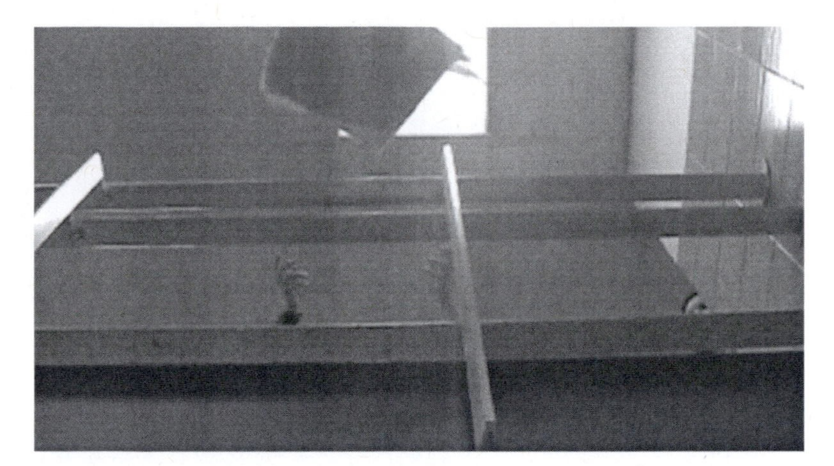

FIGURE 5.3 Mercy drops the collected signs down the stairwell.

was an essential component to the class, commenting, "Oh, it has to be done … it lets you show off your work and have people fawn over it, but it also gives honest critique." That critique became an important part of the learning process as students became more comfortable sharing their thoughts about each other's work throughout the year.

What students learned. Mercy, who had failed English in a previous year, created a well-composed and engaging text. She worked hard to bring the project to its fruition. She was attentive to her audience, following her teacher's advice and juxtaposing various shots to maintain audience attention during long sequences. She was equally attentive to the types of shots she included and worked to arrange each so they would be impactful. She elicited the help of the class, teachers, and friends by including them in the video. She recorded the voice-over for the video several times before she used it in her video, making sure she was satisfied with the dramatic reading she gave it. The other focal students in the class worked equally hard, overcoming various obstacles as they worked to achieve their vision for the film. While each student learned valuable technological skills—from filming, importing video onto the computer, and editing the video within iMovie—they also learned compositional skills that are transferable to other academic work. Students spent a considerable amount of time editing their voice-overs, recording and re-recording them, paying careful attention to the way they sounded when read out loud. They also spent considerable time editing each shot, often asking for their peers' feedback to ensure they were getting it just right. This kind of attention, purposefulness, and collaboration are too often missing from traditional classroom spaces. Participation in this project allowed students to *think* and *act* like storytellers.

As storytellers, students drew upon their background knowledge of music videos, employing genres, narrative structures, production aesthetics, and other aspects of the form to engage with life philosophies, ideas, concepts and, viewpoints culled from their experiences. Though the story was being told through digital video, they worked with a variety of media. While the images and sounds they worked with were compelling, students' work with the written word during this project was compelling, as well. Students engaged in a considerable amount of writing, often editing and working through multiple drafts. In this sense, the digital video project engaged them more deeply as readers and writers than their previous traditional English courses had.

What Students Need for Effortful Attention to Texts

Time to Make It Work

From start to finish the music video project took just over 30 class periods to complete. For many teachers this may seem like a long time to devote to one project. However, the amount of learning that took place during the unit is evident in the completed videos. Mercy's video, which served as an example here, reflects the purposeful consideration of audience and message, of showing instead of telling, and an attention to detail most English teachers would be thrilled to see in their own students' work. The community of learning that supported student meaning making throughout the unit needed this time to develop. The class periods Joel devoted to sharing and talking about student writing, the rough drafts of their videos and their final products provided opportunities for the kind of reflection, sharing, and discussion that Applebee (2002) and Langer (2000) argue are essential components of successful English instruction.

A Social Process for Making Sense and Making Meaning

How can this glimpse inside a New Literacies Classroom help English teachers successfully incorporate digital video composing into their teaching? First, it is important to note that many of the activities students engaged in are regular features of English Language Arts. Students wrote, revised, and shared their writing. They discussed their writing with one another, providing constructive feedback, taking up the identities of readers, writers—and filmmakers. Making the video brought them back to and extended their writing, giving it a deeper meaning, a place to be in the world, as they worked to capture their ideas on film using visual images, music, and voice-over narration.

Joel's instructional strategies supported student learning. Joel frontloaded the assignment by asking students to write about their lives, engaging them in an opportunity to reflect on songs that were important to them. This rooted the work they were doing in terms of their own personal experiences. He created curricular space in his classrooms for students to share this writing, entering into this community of writers by sharing his own work with his students. In this way Joel positioned himself as a more experienced other (Vygotsky, 1978), modeling the kind of writing students might engage in for their project. Joel provided other models as well, by having students read Nick Hornsby's essay and view several music videos in class. In each case he talked with his students about these texts, asking for their responses and engaging them in short discussions about how each video was composed. Joel employed the process approach to writing in his class, conferencing with students and providing ongoing support as they took their initial journal writing through several drafts before recording them for use in their videos. It was this conferencing that seemed to provide the most important instructional support for students. By meeting with each student on a regular basis, Joel was able to work with his students at their individual point of need, offering suggestions and working with them to overcome the various obstacles they encountered as they developed their projects.

Learning and meaning making became public and social in Joel's classroom. By asking students to share their work in progress with the class and by facilitating a conversation around that work, Joel provided the kind of forum for feedback and sharing found in successful communities of learning. Joel used deadlines as a means of supporting student learning, extending them when appropriate and providing a cushion between the deadline and the film screenings in class. This allowed him to begin a new unit, but also provided students with an opportunity to finish their videos on their own time before the class screenings. In this sense, deadlines were reworked to provide students with additional time, but to also allow Joel the opportunity to begin a new unit. The in-class film screenings were another essential component to the unit, providing a publication space for student work, an important component of the process approach to writing instruction. Coupled with the personal nature of the assignment, it gave further purpose to the project.

The process Joel followed for this project, which became a regular feature of the class throughout the year, was a stark contrast to the typical assignment flow chart found in many ELA classrooms where the teacher assigns a writing topic and a due date, collects the writing on the assigned date, assesses the writing, and returns that writing to the students with some feedback. In contrast, Joel worked at ground level with his students—supporting them at their individual points of need, keenly aware of the work they were engaged in. He provided ongoing feedback as they progressed through the unit. The digital video composing project allowed students to mobilize their prior experiences and engagement with popular culture. In this sense, popular culture jump-started the learning and meaning making students engaged in, providing them with an opportunity to connect traditional forms of writing with their lived experiences. Creating a digital video afforded students the opportunity to become content producers, as they worked with multiple forms of media to tell their stories for a real audience.

The process described here serves as an overview of how Joel approached instruction in his classroom, how he supported student learning, and how we might take up these practices to engage students in similar meaning making in our own classroom. While many of us may not have the time or the curricular space Joel enjoyed in "Mass Media and Video Productions," a similar project may extend from any literature or inquiry unit. In this instance, teachers might encourage students to pick up on the larger ideas, themes, and issues studied in, for example, *Of Mice and Men* (or any work of literature). They then might ask their students to write about one of these themes, connecting it to the novella *and to their own lives.* From there they could follow Joel's approach and ask students to choose a song that connects to their writing, composing a journal about the song and the role it has played in their lives. Students could then turn that writing into a music video project similar to the project described in this chapter. In this way students are given an opportunity to write about the literature they have read, connect that literature to their own lives, and extend their thinking through the literacy opportunities digital video composing affords.

The digital revolution has occurred, and the students in our classrooms have been shaped by it. As English teachers we must understand our students and what they are capable of doing given the right pedagogical practices and curricular designs. Their work in the world should guide us as we seek a new relevancy for our English classrooms, one centered on powerful literacies, both print and digital, and one that is always social and rooted in our students' lived experiences.

References

Applebee, A. N. (2002). Engaging students in the disciplines of English: What are effective schools doing? *The English Journal, 91*(6), 30–36.

Bailey, N. M. (2009). 'It makes it more real': Teaching new literacies in a secondary English classroom. *English Education, 41*(3), 207–234.

Borowicz, S. (2005). *Embracing lives through the video lens: An exploration of literacy teaching and learning with digital video technology in an urban secondary English classroom.* Unpublished doctoral dissertation, University at Buffalo, Buffalo, NY.

Bruce, D. L. (2009). Writing with visual images: Examining the video composition processes of high school students. *Research in the Teaching of English, 43*(4), 426–450.

Cercone, J. (2010). Learning English in new times: The participatory design spaces of the new literacies classroom. Unpublished doctoral dissertation, University at Buffalo, Buffalo, NY.

Costello, A. (2010). Silencing stories: The triumphs and tensions of multimodal teaching and learning in an urban context. In P. Albers & J. Sanders (Eds.), *Literacies, the arts and multimodality* (pp. 234–254). Urban, IL: National Council of Teachers of English.

Hull, G. A. (2003). Youth culture and digital media: New literacies for new times. *Research in the Teaching of English, 38*(2), 229–233.

Hull, G. A., & Nelson, M. E. (2005). Locating the semiotic power of multimodality. *Written Communication, 22*(2), 224–261.

Jenkins, H., Purushotma, R., Weigel, M., Clinton, K., & Robison, A. (2009). *Confronting the challenges of participatory culture: Media education for the 21st century.* Cambridge, MA: MIT Press.

Langer, J. A. (2000). Guidelines for teaching middle and high school students to read and write well: Six features of effective instruction. *National Research Center on English Learning and Achievement*. Retrieved from http://www.eric.ed.gov/PDFS/ED462679.pdf

Lankshear, C., & Bigum, C. (1999). Literacies and new technologies in school settings. *Pedagogy, Culture and Society*, 7(3), 445–465.

Miller, S. M. (2007). English teacher learning for new times: Digital video composing as multimodal literacy practice. *English Education*, *40*(1), 61–83.

Miller, S. M. (2008). Teacher learning for new times: Repurposing new multimodal literacies and digital-video composing for schools. In J. Flood, S. B. Heath, & D. Lapp (Eds.), *Handbook of research on teaching literacy through the communicative and visual arts* (Vol. 2, pp. 441–460). New York: Erlbaum and the International Reading Association.

Literacies, the arts and multimodality (pp. 254–281). Urban, IL: National Council of Teachers of English.

Ranker, J. (2008a). Making meaning on the screen: Digital video production about the Dominican Republic. *Journal of Adolescent & Adult Literacy* *51*(5), 410–422.

Ranker, J. (2008b). Composing across multiple media: A case study of digital video production in a fifth grade classroom. *Written Communication*, *25*(2), 196–234.

Vygotsky. L. S. (1978). *Mind in society: The development of higher psychological processes* Cambridge, Cambridge, MA: Harvard University Press.

Wilhelm, J. D., Hackett, J. D., & Baker, T .N. (2002). *Strategic reading: Guiding students to lifelong literacy, 6-12*. New York: Heinemann.

6

ENGAGING LITERATURE THROUGH DIGITAL VIDEO COMPOSING

A Teacher's Journey to "Meaning that Matters"

Monica Blondell and Suzanne M. Miller

In a time of so much talk about improving education, it is ironic that educational policies are inconsistent with what we know about learning in the digital age. National agendas emphasize standardized content-area knowledge, "back-to-the-basics" and "one-size-fits-all" curriculum (Lankshear & Bigum, 1999; McCracken, 2004). States label schools as failing to transmit factual knowledge (e.g., Hirsch, 1987), as reflected in scores on required state exams. Teachers and students have a small or no role in educational reform—the acts of teaching and learning are reduced to "technical activities devoid of artistry" and agency (DiPardo et al., 2006; Dudley-Marling, 2005; Fecho, 2003).

In contrast, a growing body of scholarship on classrooms that incorporate multimodal literacies into the curriculum demonstrates the powerful expansion of teaching, learning and teacher-student agency possible in schools. In this chapter we provide a descriptive account of one teacher as she learned to integrate digital video (DV) composing as a tool for learning the English curriculum in her 10th- and 11th-grade urban classroom—while at the same time—she navigated demands for traditional schooling and teaching to high-stakes tests.

Big Ideas to Explain the Need for Change

Humans have always used many modes beyond print to communicate and represent—think of cave paintings and varied musical styles like jazz and the waltz. But 21st-century technologies provide the digital means to represent and communicate meaning *easily* through multiple modes—the visual, audio, gestural, and spatial. This attention to multimodal literacies challenges traditional theories of communication and meaning-making as static, print-based, always and everywhere the same (e.g., New London Group, 1996, 2000; Cope & Kalantzis, 2000; Street, 1996).

As explained by social semiotic theories (Kress, 2003, 2010), the move away from the 20th-century domination of only print-based texts occurred because communication has changed, now requiring the orchestration of images, sounds, movements and print. In these multimodally designed texts—evident everywhere from web pages to cell phone screens and YouTube videos—users are foregrounded as active participants in creating and adapting ways of expression to realize their intended meanings. For example, in the process of digital video composing, now a broadly accessible multimodal literacy, all of these modes are readily available (e.g., image, gesture, speech, writing, color, music, movement) for *designing* meaning.

New literacies Studies (NLS) serves as an integrative approach to these multimodal theories and provides a useful educational lens on the literacy practices emerging from the new texts and uses of texts in 21st-century contexts (Alvermann, 2002, 2010; Gee, 2004; Lankshear & Knobel, 2003, 2006). Although literacies have always been multiple and cultural, technological advances and globalization have accelerated access to and audiences for these literacy practices. Over the last decade, adolescents increasingly use emerging literacies with multimodal texts in their everyday lives. Yet they rarely have opportunities to use them for school learning. Why? Some blame teachers who do not understand these communicative changes (e.g., Prensky, 2001); others blame schools as rigid status quo organizations (e.g., O'Brien & Bauer, 2005). Increasingly, researchers and educators call on learning institutions to recognize and include emerging literacies to engage learners in activities geared towards full and active citizenship and workplace effectiveness in the present and future. If school practices could allow students to bring their knowledge of multimodal literacies into the classroom, many benefits to individuals and society might accrue through authentic uses of new literacies in learning the curriculum.

Ms. Gorski Tries DV Composing with Students

Through our Digital Video Composing project,[1] we worked with urban teachers who wanted to integrate digital video composing into their classrooms, we saw classes that hummed with energy and some that didn't. We watched students suddenly come to life, and a few who still sat in the corner, apparently asleep (e.g., Miller, 2010). We were interested in how things might change for teachers and students over time when teachers tried student DV composing as a learning tool.

The School and the Teacher

We met Diane Gorski at our Digital Video Composing professional development (8 Saturday morning sessions). At first Diane was skeptical, uncertain that making videos would reach her urban students. But she was moved by how engaged she felt in making her own videos that enlisted her students as actors. Curious about how students would respond to making *their* own videos, she tried one small project. At the beginning of the next school year, Monica asked to watch Diane's students compose their first video that year. She visited and stayed for a year to watch Diane and her students at work. Monica wanted to answer the question, what happens over time when an urban teacher designs and enacts digital video projects as part of her high school English classroom?

Tower School, where Diane taught, was part of an urban district in a middle-sized working-class city in the Northeast. The district and school were considered by the state as in need of improvement, with attendance rates at 78% (93% state average) and below average performance level on state tests. The student population had 41% African Americans, 34% Latino, 14% Asian, 9% white, with 34% English learners and 78% free/reduced lunch. Only 53% of students graduated from high school. Although the school seemed to support teachers by offering common planning period for content area teachers, frequent unannounced classroom evaluations by district administrators monitoring adherence to mandated pedagogy and curriculum created tension in the school.

An African American, Diane Gorski had 7 years teaching experience at the time of the study. She participated in the professional development institute in November 2006 and attended roundtables and reunions where teachers collectively discussed project ideas, the possibilities and limitations of student DV composing for learning curriculum, and the struggles and challenges of integrating DV in the high-stakes testing context. In 2008, she presented her work at the local DV composing conference, providing a window on how she talked about her reflection and learning in a professional community. She taught 11th-grade English, the year of state graduation testing, which provided the chance to see how she navigated the district-required test preparation with DV composing activities.

The Process of Learning to Integrate

The larger study (Blondell, 2009) traced Diane's ongoing reflection about multimodal composing, student engagement (and teacher engagement), and learning curriculum. Over time, her questions persisted as she looked for ways she could revise her teaching in general and specifically how she could adapt future projects. This inquiry contributed to critical junctures (Holland, Lachicotte, Skinner, & Cain, 1998) about changing her role and identity in the classroom to provide meaningful learning opportunities for her students. In what follows we focus on a few of Diane's critical junctures to tell the story of her change (see Figure 6.1).

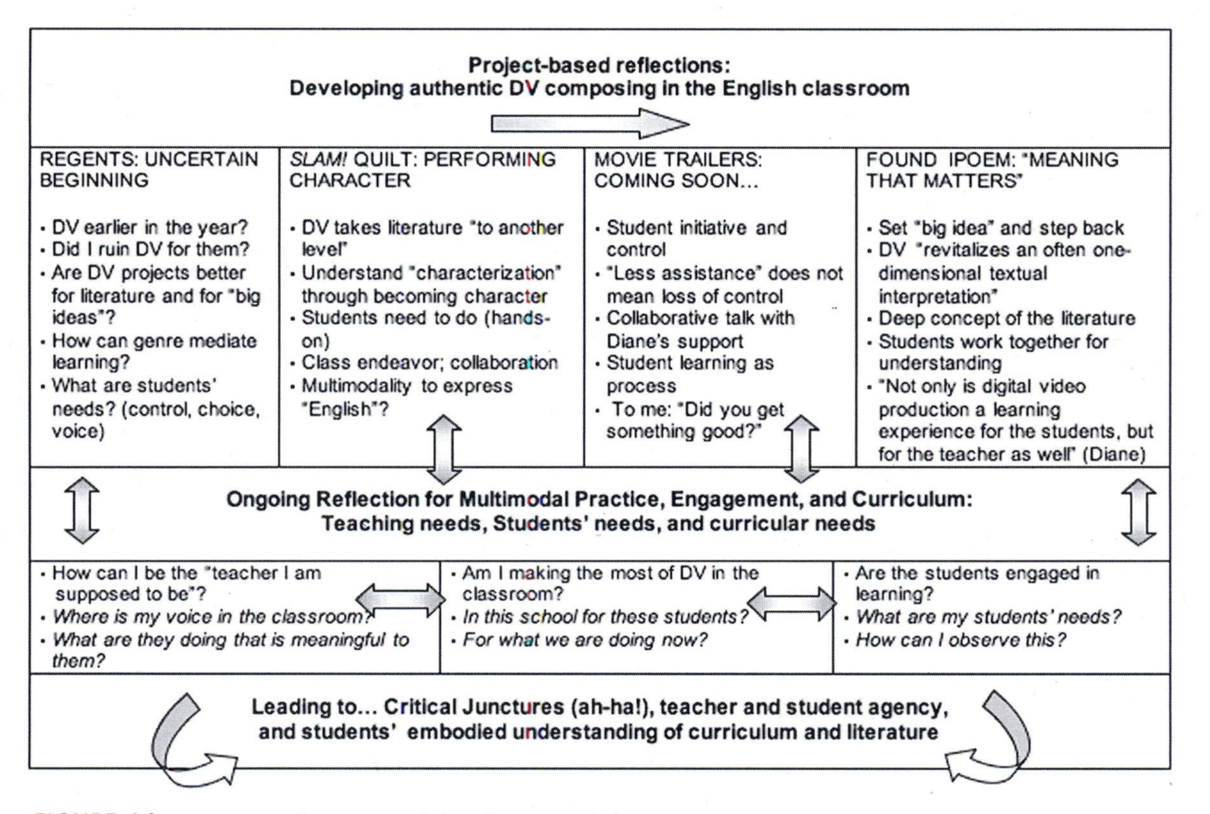

FIGURE 6.1 Trajectory of Diane Gorski's reflection and change

Diane's Inquiry into Finding a Way to Change

In conversation and interviews, Diane revealed her struggle: "How can I be the 'teacher I am supposed to be'?" Where is my voice in the classroom in this school and for these students? Are the students engaged in learning? What are they doing that is meaningful to them? How can they get something out of school that they will take with them? These questions arose over the year and centered eventually on how her students could "explore and love literature like I do."

An uncertain beginning. Diane wanted to allow students to "get their feet wet" with the idea of planning and constructing a DV product. She felt her students were having difficulties expressing their own ideas in writing, especially on the state graduation test essays with their emphasis on a controlling idea and thematic lens. Diane also noticed that students had difficulty understanding how they were going to be evaluated on the essays. She thought the language of the essay rubrics was impersonal and students had difficulty connecting the formal labels to their own writing: "It was their first DV of the year and I wanted to do something that would help them or remind them of what they need to do on the [state exam] and basically let 'em know what they'd be rated on." She saw DV as a possible tool for student learning: by composing a DV on these test rubric qualities, they would interpret the criteria using their "own language" and then create their understanding using all the available modes in DV.

Diane felt that the uncommercial genre—selling an idea—would be most appropriate because the editing and length were simple for those unfamiliar with the DV software, and students already knew the structures of ads. By the end of the second day, all groups had completed several sentences in their own words that represented their assigned quality (e.g., organization, details, etc.), yet students weren't engaging with the project in the way that she had hoped. As Diane saw what students were producing without her constant and direct help, though, her perspective on teaching began to change.

She couldn't "give them" the content if they were writing the script. Yet, that is what, at first, her students wanted—to be told what to do. Most had come from years of traditional rote learning experiences and struggled with coming up with their own ideas. Instead of merely handing them a final product, though, Diane wanted to offer resources, props, and ideas that would help them create their final project, as teachers in the project professional development described. In her interview, she recalled: "The students worked in the groups on their own and we just helped them with the technology, getting familiar with it and how to import things and how to juggle things around." She was there, she told students, to help with "whatever you guys need."

Emerging new roles. Diane first seemed to become aware of her new role in the day-to-day adaptations she made during the introduction of the project. She came to see, as she said, that DV composing relied more on "student creativity" than on teacher authority. She saw how she needed to help resituate and redefine the class space as one that relied upon student participation and collaboration. Both the role of the teacher and the role of students were challenged by the project. Especially after the final screening, Diane observed the "really good projects" were made when there was less direct assistance from her.

On the other hand, while the students were creating their commercials, Diane became concerned that the projects were taking too long and the students were losing interest: "I just hate the project, maybe I shouldn't have done it." She mentioned in our informal conversations that students weren't as "into it" as she hoped they would be. Although she had student engagement in mind, the project was firmly focused on state curriculum. Diane paid close attention to her students throughout the rubric commercial project, trying to figure out how she could make projects better for her students. Her desire was to adapt so that she could "bring students in":

> [Teachers] have to find the way to bring the students in. Um, there's, it's well known in education that if your students aren't involved, part of it may be the students, part of it may be you, [you] need to reassess how it is that you're teaching and what you're doing to get the students into whatever it is, whatever content area it is.

Diane's continual reference to finding "the way to bring the students in" shows her ongoing reflection on what kind of good teaching could engage student responsibility and ownership.

This first DV project was a challenge, but she began to reevaluate the ways DV could be used in English class. Rather than creating projects around factual content, she began to think that DV could be used as a tool to engage students in *creating* the content around the "big ideas" of English—such as characterization, symbolism, and theme. She also began to see how genre and the modes were essential to constructing spaces where students could inject their voices and visions to gain a deeper and more connected understanding of curriculum. As she adapted, she saw that students craved authentic purposes, just as she did.

Finding "Meaning that Matters"

Over the year, Diane concluded that students would feel authentic purpose if she designed DV projects around literature, directed towards their making meaning. She was pleased with the video confessionals students created dramatizing the real thoughts of characters in *Slam!* by Walter Dean Meyers. Her attention turned to how this kind of project changed students' position in the classroom even more: "It's kind of really nice for them to know that, that what they, what they think matters." In the last DV composing project of the year with her 11th graders the changes in Diane and her students' were clearly evident.

Goals for the "Found" iPoem video assignment. In her 11th-grade class she introduced a DV project related to the novel *Their Eyes Were Watching God* (Hurston, 1937/2000). Integrating DV around this particular novel was important to her, as it would give her a chance to explore one of her favorite novels—one that she loved to read and "loved to teach." She felt there was an authentic purpose when students could explore meaning from a novel rich with language, themes, and literary elements. They could approach the novel with their own knowledge, feelings, and beliefs because this novel had "so much good language" that related to their lives. Her idea about Zora Neale Hurston's language resonated with Bruner's (1986) account of how literary language could "recruit the reader's imagination" and allow for students to fill the literary "gaps" with their own meaning.

As Diane considered how best to construct the project, she knew she wanted her students to take another look at the novel and construct their own meaning by looking at it through the lens of "self-discovery," a concept that would be meaningful to her 11th graders. She had more confidence in planning because she had created and enacted projects that she'd believed were fairly successful: students had learned curriculum and the process of composing DV, and she had managed the "technology and wires." She appeared to be taking what she had learned from her prior planning and incorporating students' needs and responses as an answer to her questions.

In addition to her goal of creating a space for students to explore language and life themes, Diane wanted students to incorporate the literary elements that were required for the state exams and begin to explore poetry, which she felt opened up possibilities for students' performance of *their own* meaning. Using the found-poem genre, students could create their own interpretation by selecting the language from the novel and connecting the lines to literary elements. Diane imagined how the project could enable students to use traditional literary terms without constraining their expression of meaning and said so as she gave the assignment: "Okay, but think about a concept or a message that *you* got out of this [novel]. Here's what we're focusing on. Write a poem about it. Or come up with a poem about it. *Find* a poem about it."

She thought each student could draw on their own knowledge, understanding and emotions to create a poem: "You'll hear different lines, they'll add music and they'll all pretty much take on their own lives, so it'll be nice to see, I think." She envisioned how her goal for students to create and express a personally relevant interpretation was possible through the multiple modes of DV.

With the poetry video she was already beginning to envision students DVs, "It will be nice to see" what students create.

Communicating aesthetic reading to students. Diane introduced the project with the assignment sheet, then provided an example found line and performed her own thinking aloud with the students. In illustrating how they could select lines for their poems that would "take on their own lives," she also showed how she could then tie the literary element imagery to the line. She included both her thinking process and her reasoning for selecting a line because it was personally relevant. The words she found in the book also "point to something outside themselves" that she could connect to her own life (Rosenblatt, 1994). In short, she performed strategies for how to create the found poem and how to read literary text, as she enacted her stance towards literature to mediate student learning.

She emphasized the power of choosing lines to create a personally relevant interpretation of the broad themes that occur in literature and offered her expertise as a tool rather than as definitive: "If you need to borrow my book because it's got some things highlighted then you can. And, in fact, I will go around and if you need help, if you get stuck, I've got some areas. But again, my book has lots of lines that are underlined and highlighted and it's easy to spot." She offered her support to students and also offered her own book, picking it up to flip through the pages to show students how she had "tagged" many pages and highlighted text, another model for reading and thinking about literature aesthetically.

As the class watched several DV examples, she highlighted different ways to do poetry videos, and students asked questions about how they might be able to use similar effects or layering. For example, one poem had a voiceover of a poem throughout the movie, with moving images and still images throughout. In several places during the iPoem, the student had inserted title shots with words, some from her poem and some related, in between and over the clips. Her student Natalie liked the idea, especially because the "words were floatin" across the screen and she thought that style of text would add to the smooth tone she wanted to create in her poem. She also imagined how she could take fragments of her spoken lines to emphasize her poem's meaning (see Figure 6.2).

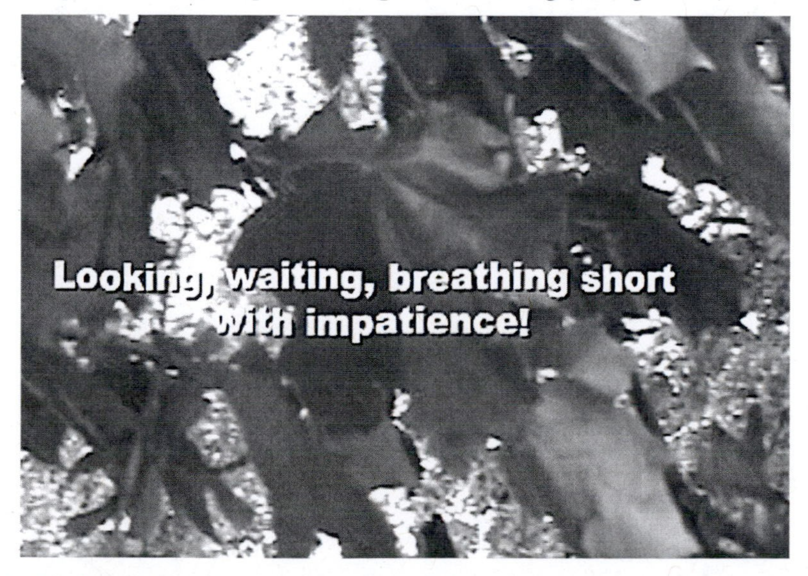

FIGURE 6.2 A frame from Natalie's poetry video

Support for the student composing process. While each group of students was finding a line from the novel to present to the class, Diane circulated to each group with her book in her hand and asked what lines were "appealing" to them. After the fourth group presented their line to the class, she said:

> Now, I can see already, like, if you are into poetry or you are into language or you want to get into language, you can see where you might go with this. And everyone can go in their own way. She was 16 [...] that idea of being 16. You guys are about 16, how do you feel? Buzzing, pears, blooming, okay. So that idea of being 16. It doesn't mean literally that she was 16, but you can make this work into a nice poem. So, I am going to step back while you are copying and thinking about your own poem.

Diane relates the line back to the students' lives and how it might relate to a poem that they would create. She encourages students to "get into language" by taking the lines to create a poem relevant to them and suggests how they could alter lines to establish a tone in their poem.

Diane knew that some of her students had never done a found poem and she expressed the "organic" process of the poem as well as how it would tie into their DV. She wanted them to begin to think about what their poems could show to illustrate their lines as well. While she was referring to the visuals that they would add during the DV composing process, she was also supporting students' visualization of the text, an important reading strategy. Although she wanted students to identify the literary elements in their poems, she did not want this to hinder their "search" for the lines; identifying the literary elements was not a "contest" or a "puzzle" meant to test them. In a sense, she was trying to demystify literature and interpretation, reminding her students, "There's no science to it. I guess, call on the gods and let the page fall where it will and be surprised." At the end of class, Diane told Monica that students had some "good insights" and that they had picked out really "fantastic" lines that would make wonderful poems.

On several days, because it was the end of the year, students were out of class for school activities. However, the found poem and the DV received continual attention by the students. Students began to come to Diane's classroom during their lunch or during study halls. Because school was almost ending, students also began to ask Diane for permission to come if they had a class where they were just watching movies or given the class time to do other work.

Initially, some students seemed to struggle with the poem and a few students would even ask Monica questions like, "Is she going to tell us what to do?" Diane again remembered that her students maybe hadn't had "opportunities to write" and to share what they were thinking in a classroom:

> I think when they realize that it's not all about what I'm going to give, you know, as a teacher, "These are the right answers and let me fill your

> head with them." It's kind of really nice for them to know that, that what they, what they think matters you know, and whatever they're going to come up with creatively, it's going to have an impact and their thoughts are of value.

Diane here sees her role as teacher as more than conveying content and her students' roles as more than remembering content. She realizes, again, that her students were unaccustomed to school activities in which a teacher emphasized that students' "thoughts were of value."

Diane connected the project to students' knowledge of cultural media to help them understand the process of creating a found poem: "It's similar to what a rapper might do now, or hip hop, what they may call sampling, is what you guys are going to do. But, I want you to think of your poems as artistic; your poems are art." She offers a familiar cultural activity, connecting to the "artistic" style of composing that counters their other school writing tasks. By repositioning students as samplers and interpreters of meaning, she provides authentic purpose.

As when she explained the guidelines to identify literary elements, Diane emphasized that her overall goal was for her students to make sense of the language in the novel, not to produce a certain procedure or answer. For example, Marcy, one of the students, said, "Miss, I'm not talkin' about self-discovery. I didn't know we were supposed to do that." Diane asked her what her poem was about and Marcy replied, "Finding love." Diane said, "Well, that's part of self-discovery, isn't it?" Marcy replied with an "mm-hmm" and went straight to work on her project. Diane here validates Marcy's idea and demonstrates that big ideas like "self-discovery" are complex and have multiple aspects.

Diane, in this project, had become aware that her role as supporter was crucial to the DV composing, and her role as authority was less apparent even as the students created their found poems. From the video footage, Diane can be heard asking questions: "Where do you see your poem going? Where are you taking it?" This was a critical juncture for Diane:

> It's amazing to see kids at work and, to me, it's about—it was about relinquishing control saying I don't—saying I don't have all the answers … Okay, so relinquishing that control, letting them do things, letting them make decisions, allowing them to discover things for themselves and just being there as a support.

Diane acknowledges here how she "stepped back" to support students and, subsequently, connects "relinquishing control" to opening up possibilities for multiple interpretations. Students explored self-discovery in the literature to express an interpretation that was valid and meaningful *to them* and exceeded Diane's expectations; students went beyond creating a meaningful DV—they made decisions and *discovered* meaning.

Student opportunities for collaborative meaning-making. As Diane took on this role, she noticed that students also began to help each other sort out their ideas about what and how they would express their vision of "search." For example, students talked about their poem's themes as they were gathering their final lines and traded lines that they liked but thought were more appropriate for another student's poem. In her interview, Diane revealed how the student collaboration was important to her and the students: "I said, 'You know what? However you guys are gonna get 'em done, you're gonna get 'em done'. And they liked working together. Then there's parts, I think, that negotiation even is cool. 'Well, no. I really want this to say this, or look like this'." In this focused conversation, students sometimes shared ideas and helped each other think of alternative ways to convey shots visually; they respected one another's ideas and helped by performing or filming for another student's DV.

Each day, Diane would begin class by stating the goals for the day such as "Let's have our poem finished by the end of today" or "You will want to have 3 or 4 shots by the end of the day." She also made it routine to announce that she would provide whatever they needed for their projects and students could use her book to find any last lines that they needed. By mid-project, it was typical for students to walk in the class and begin working. Then, about 5 minutes into class, Diane would address them all: "Hall passes? Cameras? Tapes?" to let them know that she had those materials.

As Diane told other teachers in her conference presentation, the found poem DV had exceeded her expectations, and she was amazed at the work students had done to create their DVs. Diane saw how her students were committed to the project and came in before school, during their free or lunch periods, or stayed after school to complete their projects. They took books home and made deliberate choices about the message of their poem and how they could best represent their poems in the DV. She had observed students working with each other even though each student was creating an individual DV found poem and said that student talk had contributed to the success of the project. She realized that students were "negotiating" curriculum by helping each other come closer to a representation that was related to the book while supporting each student's own interpretation and ideas.

Monica asked Diane how she thought they all ended up coming up with different meanings and different DV poems based on the same novel. Diane said:

> I almost think they don't get enough opportunities to write creatively, think creatively. I mean I thought about how many times in the past 5 years that I've been teaching English 3, have I allowed three weeks or more from beginning to end, obviously, but think about a concept or a message that you got out of this. "Here's what we're focusing on. Write a poem about it. Or come up with a poem about it. Find a poem about it." They don't get those opportunities [...] but they got to do something

> that usually I don't allow time for...need to start allowing more time for these things, obviously, because products are amazing, really. [...] Well, maybe we need to tap into the things they do at home, and maybe they'd be more interested in school, and they'd write the essays, and they'd do the thinking that we need 'em to do on the must-dos—the exams, the tests, the assessments—if we allowed for a little more of that.

Diane here realizes the role of DV in her classroom and how she had and could change her teaching to "allow time for" it throughout the year. The DV poems seem to be the point when Diane saw what was valuable in the process of DV and how it could be translated to everyday teaching and learning. The following semester, in a proposal to present at the National Council of Teachers of English annual conference, she wrote: "Ironically, the major theme of the novel itself is *discovery*. As the presentation unfolds, it becomes evident that not only is digital video production a learning experience for the students, but for the teacher as well." Her change came from close observation of the various ways that students were making sense of the curriculum in powerful *and* "academic" ways. She saw that students were more engaged and invested in the class activities and were able to represent a deep understanding of curriculum through the modes of DV and in their writing.

Changes in Teaching Leads to Changes in Learning

Seeing student learning in DV composing. Diane was amazed with the students' products and she considered what the DV projects offered for her class as a whole. In other words, she began to look at what the students did during the project that related to her class and her curriculum. In her interview, she remarked:

> I think when it's all said and done I could say that it seems like they got a deeper, a firmer grasp on literature. Hopefully—and you'd have to ask them ... my hope and what I've observed from some is that they grew to love the literature in a different way, not just superficially.

Her comments reveal how she feels the DV project provided an opportunity for students to engage in literature and also construct a different personal stance towards reading literature.

Diane's student Natalie who got good grades, but didn't usually engage deeply, echoed what Diane observed about the project:

> I think the purpose is like what Mrs. Gorski was trying to—is trying to make the English class more fun and more exciting instead of just reading books that we've been doing all year. And we read a lot of books, but I guess to further help us understand what the book is about, she makes us

> do projects and poems and all that. And it really helps me to understand the book a lot.

Natalie concurs that DV composing "really helps" her understanding of the novel. She began to see Janie as a real person with thoughts and emotions, rather than just a character. A novel wasn't only a plot with characters and a plot that could be neatly summarized and understood by answering end-of-the-chapter questions. There was more meaning to be created. To examine Diane Gorski's assessment that students had learned about the novel and literature deeply, we next explore Natalie's learning through her account of her composing of the found poem and video on *Their Eyes Were Watching God*.

The power of transmediating print. This story of change from the student's perspective provides a clear portrait of how and what Natalie learned. The activity of portraying a print text meaning in another sign system—as Natalie and other students did—is an example of *transmediating*, a semiotic concept referring to the act of translating meaning from one sign system to another (Siegel, 1995). Findings suggest that this translation generated depth of focus and opportunity for reflection as students composed/created/invented connections between the original literary text and the emerging multimodal text of the digital video.

Although Natalie was a fairly successful student in Ms. Gorski's English class, she described herself as "lazy" and "slouching all the time" when "we read books and we do the worksheets." As they began reading *Their Eyes Were Watching God*, Natalie told her teacher, "I hate this book." To ease the difficulties of reading dialect, Ms. Gorski played the audio book and stopped to discuss interpretations. Creating a "found poem" and designing a video to represent it multimodally changed the experience for Natalie. She found herself "digging deeper" into the text "'cause I wanted to know how [Janie] was feeling." Rereading and reflecting with a purpose, as an inquiry, were prompted by DV composing and her search for Janie's feelings: "Was she ready to call it quits? You couldn't just find out how that was just by reading the book and then saying, 'Yeah. I know what it was.' You have to go through certain chapters and find out what was going on with her. I think I kinda' learned from that.... You have to find deep in there and find words that helped her find love."

"Everything means something." After making her poetry video, Natalie explained the difference for her in this approach to literature: "We're reading books and we're just basically just digging more into the book and being creative with it instead of just reading a book, taking a test on it ... [DV] helps me to understand the curriculum of English."

Her reference to the "curriculum of English" was a startling formulation. She not only shares her appreciation of the novel, she expands the revelation to all novels and to what English is about. This broad reframing from an 11th-grade student about literature seems to result from time, thought, and transmediation. Her re-reading and reflection were aimed towards seeking to create images that matched the words and her sense of their meaning. She said, "I think my favorite part is when [we] took—trees blowing and all that. I liked that a lot because it kinda' matched that line when [Janie] was looking and waiting, really. It kinda' matched perfectly." This aesthetic response to the combined words and images as symbolic seemed to animate Natalie's connection to and interpretation of the book. While the credits rolled at the end, she added Ashanti's "Don't Let Them" because she thought it represented Janie's search: "Like, they say that she's a fool and she's too dumb to know what's good for her and that, you know, he needs to love her." Natalie's final musical commentary speaks to her deep understanding of Janie and, perhaps, of the position of too many women who are judged and belittled.

After making her poetry video on their *Eyes Were Watching God*, Natalie felt, "I would definitely use that on a critical lens question [state graduation exam task] because now I know a lot about the book. I've learned so much about it. And I can just right off the bat tell every single detail about the book." Because in the class students transmediated the book to a poetry video, Natalie had "spent more time with it than any other book that we've done." This lengthier consideration, she felt, prepared her better than other ways, to be able to write a timed essay on this novel. Her whole encounter with the novel appeared to be a threshold experience for Natalie: in working with her group and then directing her own video, overall Natalie learned, "Everything means something," a new vision of literature for her. For English teachers, arguably, this is the grail of student understanding—a recognition of the need for questioning the meaning of the signs in texts and all around us.

Lessons from Diane's and Natalie's Journeys

Shifting the Status of Students' Composing

Diane's transformation of goals, roles, and the status of meaning-making in her classroom occurred as she was integrating digital composing about literature by focusing on student needs and learning. As a teacher, she facilitated and learned from students. By the end of the school year, she was planning and enacting innovative practice, and relying more on students' contributions. Through her ongoing inquiry, she had been able to answer the question she first posed: "How do I give students more control?" Through her shifting role as teacher, she was also taking on a new professional identity characterized by attention to student learning as a priority. She was learning from the students about how she could transform her pedagogy in ways that would make literature learning more available and more authentic for them. This adaptive stance allowed her to constructively critique her practice, rather than feel as if she had failed when everything did not go as she had hoped and planned.

Diane was beginning to indicate a new stance towards literature learning in her class by using all the affordances of DV composing to enhance this learning. The students were invited to construct meaning from literature, rather than merely locate the meaning buried beneath terminology and authoritative knowledge. In this way, Diane became aware that an authentic purpose could enable deep engagement around curricular concepts. She observed how students became more active, coming up with ideas or "going to get a book" from her bookshelf all on their own. She saw the importance of initiating social transactions with her students that made apparent that they could and should take on these active leadership roles. Her interactions with students, as she was seeing and encouraging authentic learning, became more collaborative, rather than directive and authoritative. Content knowledge was changing from something that was studied to something that was created and discovered. In Feire's (1970/2000) terms, students moved from being objects that received knowledge to subjects who posed problems and composed their knowing through dialogue and many modes.

A Lifeline for Diane

"So this is why I teach." When she attended the professional development on DV composing, Diane was searching for a way to renew her teaching. She felt beaten down by the "downtowners," the upper administrators in her urban school district who monitored the mandated direct instruction and test-prep curriculum. When Diane could teach as the "teacher I was supposed to be," she provided more authentic spaces for student learning and began to re-see what students were doing as meaningful—for the curriculum and beyond her class. When she could create a project about self-discovery for one of her favorite novels, she found a life-line—"Ok, so this is why I teach. These students were proud of their work and will remember it."

Like Diane, all teachers need to "see" and "hear" student interest, engagement and learning. Over time, she developed strategies for examining the process of student learning—mainly talking with them and asking questions as they made decisions. In the screenings when students like Natalie their videos and their thinking, she saw their commitment to making sense and communicating.

Felt purpose. This is what Diane came to know over the school year when she introduced DV composing to her students and learned to support their needs to understand, to represent, to communicate: she came to see herself and her students in the same situation, since students, too, needed to feel purpose and meaningfulness in the work that they do. In their DV composing, with Diane's support, her students were afforded a space to construct their own meaning, using many layered modes to represent and communicate their understanding.

They owned the curriculum and, in turn, the novel, and the main character Janie. The range of projects that came from this authentic inquiry suggests that one size never fits all. School activities, DV or not, need to be geared towards students as constructors of meaning—only then will students understand the curriculum in a deep way.

Note

1. City Voices, City Visions (CVCV) was a partnership between the University at Buffalo Graduate School of Education and the Buffalo Public Schools (BPS), over 260 urban teachers have participated in CVCV professional development institutes aimed at preparing subject-area teachers to use DV composing as a new multimodal literacies tool for their 6th- to 12th-grade urban students. See www.CityVoicesCityVisions.org for more information.

References

Alvermann, D. E. (Ed.). (2002). *Adolescents and literacies in a digital world.* New York: Peter Lang.

Alvermann, D. E. (Ed.). (2010). *Adolescents online literacies: Connecting classrooms, digital media, and popular culture.* New York: Peter Lang.

Blondell, M. (2009). *An English teacher's design of digital video composing in an urban high school: Impacts on student learning and engagement.* Unpublished doctoral dissertation, University at Buffalo, State University of New York.

Bruner, J. S. (1986). *Actual minds, possible worlds.* Cambridge, MA: Harvard University Press.

Cope, B., & Kalantzis, M. (2000). Multiliteracies: The beginning of an idea. In B. Cope & M. Kalantzis (Eds.), *Multiliteracies: Literacy learning and the design of social futures* (pp. 3–8). London: Routledge.

DiPardo, A. Whitney, A., Fleischer, C., Johnson, T S., Mayher, J., McCracken, N., et al. (2006). Understanding the relationship between research and teaching. *English Education, 38,* 295–311.

Dudley-Marling, C. (2005). Disrespecting teachers: Troubling developments in reading instruction. *English Education, 37*(4), 272–279.

Fecho, B. (2003). *"Is this English?": Race, language, and culture in the classroom.* New York: Teachers College Press.

Freire, P. (1970/2000). *Pedagogy of the Oppressed.* (M. B. Ramos, Trans.; 30th Anniversary ed.) New York: Continuum International.

Gee, J. P. (2004). *Situated language and learning.* New York: Routledge.

Hirsch, E. D. (1987). *Cultural literacy: What every American needs to know.* Boston: Houghton Mifflin.

Holland, D., Lachicotte, W., Skinner, D., & Cain, C. (1998). *Identity and agency in cultural worlds.* Cambridge, MA: Harvard University Press.

Hurston, Z. N. (1937/2000). *Their eyes were watching God.* New York: Harper Collins.

Kress, G. (2003). *Literacy in the new media age.* New York: Routledge.

Kress, G. (2010). *Multimodality: A social semiotic view of contemporary communication.* New York: Routledge.

Lankshear, C., & Bigum, C. (1999). Literacies and new technologies in school settings. *Pedagogy, Culture & Society,* 7(3), 445–465. Retrieved from http://dx.doi.org/10.1080/14681369900200068

Lankshear, C., & Knobel, M. (2003). *New literacies: Changing knowledge and the classroom.* Buckingham, UK: Open University Press.

Lankshear, C., & Knobel, M. (2006). *New literacies: Everyday practices and classroom learning* (second edition). Maidenhead, UK: Open University Press.

McCracken, N. M. (2004). Surviving shock and awe: NCLB vs. college of education. *English Education, 34*, 214–236.

Miller, S. M. (2010). Reframing multimodal composing for student learning: *Lessons on Purpose from the Buffalo DV project. Contemporary Issues in Technology And Teacher Education, 10*(2). Retrieved from http://www.citejournal.org/vol10/iss2/maintoc.cfm

Myers, W. D. (1996). *Slam!* New York: Scholastic.

New London Group. (1996). A pedagogy of multiliteracies: Designing social futures. *Harvard Educational Journal, 66*(1), 60–92.

New London Group. (2000). A pedagogy of multiliteracies: Designing social futures. In B. Cope & M. Kalantzis (Eds.), *Multiliteracies: Literacy learning and the design of social futures* (pp. 9–38). London: Routledge.

O'Brien, D. G., & Bauer, E. B. (2005). New literacies and the institution of old learning. *Reading Research Quarterly, 40*(1), 120–131.

Prensky, M. (2001). Digital natives, digital immigrants. *On the Horizon, 9*(5), 1–2. Retrieved from http://www.marcprensky.com/writing/Prensky%20-%20Digital%20Natives,%20Digital%20Immigrants%20-%20Part1.pdf

Rosenblatt, L. M. (1994). *The reader, the text, the poem: The transactional theory of the literary work.* Carbondale: South Illinois University Press. (Original work published 1978)

Siegel, M. (1995). More than words: The generative power of transmediation for learning. *Canadian Journal of Education, 20*(4), 455–475.

Street, B. (1996). *Social literacies: Critical approaches to literacy development, ethnography and education.* London: Longman.

7

LESSONS IN MULTIMODAL COMPOSITION FROM A FIFTH-GRADE CLASSROOM

Lynn E. Shanahan

Recent developments in the use of digital technologies within society have created a convergence of print-based text and electronic texts. Some have argued that the convergence of technologies—for example, engaging students in the composition of text that includes graphics, video, images, and audio signs—has the potential to have more of an impact within education than previous technologies (MacArthur, 2006). On the other hand, some educators are skeptical, noting that in the past people had predicted that the then new technologies of radio or television would radically alter schooling. You might be asking: How are recent technology changes any different from what has gone on before? Are these changes really transformative or are they just the typical response to new technologies?

Unlike other technologies that were once considered new, such as radio or television, digital technologies afford users opportunity to easily and quickly integrate different sign systems to compose multimodal texts. Although composing multimodally with digital technologies is an exciting possibility, it often runs counter to assumptions of print communications that have informed teachers' beliefs and classroom instruction. That is, like the rest of us, most teachers have formed their knowledge and understandings of literacy around the printed word in the schools they attended and in the schools where they now educate children. These current changes in digital technologies and our apprenticeship with print-based literacies require that literacy researchers and educators further examine ways to support students and teachers in their acquisition of necessary skills and strategies to write with digital technologies (International Reading Association [IRA], 2009).

This chapter focuses on the composition of multimodal texts in a fifth-grade science unit where students investigated the impact of acid rain on ecological systems. The teacher and students used HyperStudio (http://www.mackiev.com/hyperstudio/), a multimedia program that uses hyperlinks between electronic pages and affords composers the opportunity to communicate multimodally using visuals, sound, and print. In exploring multimodal texts, I consider the questions: What happens when a motivated fifth-grade teacher who has a traditional print-based focus on literacy uses digital technologies for students to compose multimodal texts? In what ways does the teacher's perspective on literacy shape how her students communicate with various sign systems?

Classroom Context and Teacher Stance

The context for this study was a unit Mrs. Bowie taught during the science block at Landers Elementary School (a pseudonym) in a small suburban district outside a northeastern city. Mrs. Bowie had taught for 13 years, and at the time of this study, she had just decided to switch grade levels and teach fifth instead of third grade. When I first began visiting her class, Mrs. Bowie indicated that she had minimal knowledge of how to communicate multimodally with digital technologies, but she stated that she wanted to "jump in" with technology integration because it was "essential for our students today." Mrs. Bowie chose to "start small" with technology integration by incorporating the digital technology into one science unit on acid rain. Similar to many teachers in the surrounding area, she had an interest in technology integration, but most of her professional development had focused on "how to use" different software programs, not on how to communicate multimodally.

When planning for the integration of technology, one area of concern for Mrs. Bowie was the amount of time it would take for 23 students to complete the composition of the multimodal text if she only used the six computers in her classroom. Consequently, she also used the bank of 25 computers in the library to ease the pressure of time. Mrs. Bowie, like many other teachers, was also preparing her students for a state science test and felt a strong sense of responsibility for their achievement.

Mrs. Bowie's actions in the classroom demonstrated her beliefs in a learner-centered environment. The classroom context was one where students collaboratively worked on solving problems with Mrs. Bowie. For example, when they were adding animations to their HyperStudio projects, she had a student demonstrate a shortcut. She knew when it came to technology use that in many cases her students were more technologically savvy than she. Mrs. Bowie intentionally positioned herself so she was not viewed as the only resource in the classroom: students asked each other questions, used resources around the room, and consulted with other educators in the building. For example, one day when students were working in partners at the computer, two students could not find a picture to represent their idea, so they asked Mrs. Bowie if they could go see Mrs. Jauch, the enrichment specialist, who had previously taught them how to use digital drawing tools. Upon finding Mrs. Jauch, the students and Mrs. Bowie participated as learners in Mrs. Jauch's mini-lesson.

Not only did Mrs. Bowie understand the value of collaborative problem solving, she also understood the pedagogical value of modeling. She began the project by modeling her expectations in the library. She chose the library because she had access to a computer with Internet access that was connected to a projector. When she modeled, students sat with great anticipation waiting for the lessons to begin. As she introduced the project, she modeled such concepts as how to access the bookmarked web sites_and how to add color to their story cards. When she was not modeling, she moved between groups supporting student learning in concepts such as how to insert scroll bars, how to add animations, and how to link story cards.

Above all, Mrs. Bowie was a reflective teacher who adapted her teaching plans to respond to the students' needs in both short and long range planning. For instance, Mrs. Bowie had not intended to teach the students how to toggle back and forth between Microsoft Word and a web site when gathering information, but adjusted her lesson when the need arose. More substantively, as students progressed through the acid rain unit, Mrs. Bowie reflected on what she would need to do to help her future students and the changes she could make the following year to improve use and integration of technology across multiple content areas, including a use of technology within the reading and writing block.

Overview of the Acid Rain Project

Mrs. Bowie placed the students into four research teams consisting of six students. Once in their groups of six, students decided who would be their partner. Two partners studied acid rain from a chemist's, biologist's, and economist's perspectives. The students used preselected Internet sites about acid rain chosen by Mrs. Bowie to engage in a Webquest. Then, they reported the effects of acid rain on the environment using HyperStudio software. In HyperStudio, students created the hyperlinks between pages, drew pictures, pasted images, wrote with text and included sounds in each stack of electronic pages. Each student group composed a home card (i.e., the first card of the stack of cards in the program) and story cards (i.e., all the cards besides the home card in the stack).

Meet the Student Research Teams

The primary participants in this study came from fifth-grade classes located in a predominantly middle-class suburb. All students demonstrated proficiency when using print-based texts and negotiating the Discourse of school (Gee, 1991), and all students read at or above grade level.

Jeremy and Danielle partnered together to study acid rain from an economist's perspective. While Danielle read on a seventh-grade reading level and Jeremy on a fifth-grade reading level, Jeremy's familiarity with technology exceeded Danielle's. Their diverse strengths caused tensions at times since Danielle did not always trust Jeremy's technological knowledge, even though it was comprehensive. At times I could hear Jeremy pleading: "Can I have the mouse, please? Come on, I can do it quickly." Then I would see Danielle clutching the mouse and staring intently at the screen. Jeremy, the least proficient student among the participants in the study with regard to reading and writing print-based text, also dealt with Attention Deficit Hyperactivity Disorder.

Krystal and April partnered to study acid rain from a chemist's perspective. Both Krystal and April read at a fifth-grade level. Krystal could be observed dancing, tapping her feet, and singing throughout the project. Krystal loved working on artistic, creative projects and enjoyed having the opportunity to draw through the multimodal composition. She preferred expressing herself through visual design elements, while her partner, April, was drawn more to representing information both linguistically and visually. As April and Krystal collaborated, they often discussed the best sign systems to represent their content.

John and Abigail collaborated on the acid rain project from a biologist's perspective. Both John and Abigail read on a seventh-grade level. According to Mrs. Bowie, John and Abigail's academic work was among the highest in the grade level. They proficiently navigated the school context both socially and academically. Both enjoyed working with electronic and print-based texts. According to a student-constructed sociogram, other students in the class preferred to work with either John or Abigail on a project. This could be attributed to the fact that both performed well academically and interacted well socially with their peers.

In the next sections I address several key ideas about multimodal text composition with digital technologies in the class through the Designs of Meaning framework developed by the NLG (New London Group, 1996): (a) how Mrs. Bowie drew upon pre-existing genres to shape the students' multimodal text composition, (b) how Mrs. Bowie positioned linguistic and visual sign systems, (c) how students used audio signs, and (d) how her instruction impacted the students' designs.

Drawing Upon Pre-existing Genres to Shape New Genres

Mrs. Bowie decided to unveil the Acid Rain Project to the students in the library because as mentioned, she would have access to a video projector and 25 computers. In the carpeted whole group meeting area the students sat with great anticipation as she introduced the Acid Rain Project. Mrs. Bowie began her explanation by describing how the students should be thinking about

HyperStudio multimodal genre as "being like a movie." She explained, "You want to use the information to create a pretty movie, if you want to call it that, to help kids learn about acid rain." Here, first Mrs. Bowie drew a parallel between a pre-existing text (a movie) that was a familiar genre to the students and the HyperStudio multimodal composition, a newer genre, thus establishing a social, historical link between texts. Although unaware of work by the NLG (1996) and Kress (1998), Mrs. Bowie emphasized a key feature of textual composition: when texts are designed, they are connected to previously established texts.

Second, in order for the students to create a "pretty movie to learn about acid rain," Mrs. Bowie indicated that students needed to draw on the semiotic conventions associated with the genre of a movie. The configuration of semiotic systems used in a movie place an emphasis on the combined use of visual, auditory, and linguistic semiotic sign systems. Movies, as a genre, rely on linguistic design elements, but emphasis is placed more on oral language, and less on written language. Thus, Mrs. Bowie positioned design elements of the written word as less prominent within this multimodal composition. Conversely, her comparison placed the visual and auditory sign systems in the foreground when she drew this parallel. Third, Mrs. Bowie purposefully used the adjective "pretty" to describe the movie and indicate the aesthetic nature of the multimodal project she wanted the children to create and to indicate her desire for children to engage the reader affectively.

Mrs. Bowie drew another parallel between a previous social studies project and the HyperStudio multimodal composition where the students had used their visual literacy (visual mode) to create banners and had orally (linguistic mode) presented information that pertained to a state they had studied. Notice how Mrs. Bowie positions the use of visual and linguistic signs in her discussion with the students.

> Think of our banners from our state projects that Mrs. Christina did a great job of teaching you how to do it—fun, but has to be informative. Words are important, but they are not as important as visuals. For me, personally, I would think you would rather see visuals than words, especially on a home card. Maybe buttons [In HyperStudio, buttons link one slide to another] bring you places that teach you things where the words are.

In the description, Mrs. Bowie directly stated that the "words are important but not as important as visuals." This comment revealed how Mrs. Bowie placed the visual sign system in the foreground and the linguistic sign system, specifically the written word, in the background. Mrs. Bowie's examples of the movie and the social studies banner project, illustrated the importance of combining visual form and oral language as means of communication when composing multimedia compositions. The examples Mrs. Bowie drew on of already existing texts were used with the intent of shaping the new text, the HyperStudio multimodal compositions.

In the social studies example, Mrs. Bowie reiterated the message that one purpose of the visual design elements was to engage the reader affectively and to lead the reader to the information provided by linguistic design elements; she stated the presentations had to be "fun, but informative." She pointed out that the linguistic elements taught the reader the content, a process that drew from the readers' cognitive engagement. Conversely, the visual designs, (images on the home card) would be more appealing and fun, which drew from the readers' affective engagement. After Mrs. Bowie's initial introduction, where she linked the HyperStudio multimodal composition to previous genres, her instruction shifted to the arrangement of signs in their writing.

Positioning Modes of Communication

According to the NLG (1996), the style of a design focuses on how the writer of the text arranges the different semiotic signs (e.g., print, images) on the screen. Because Mrs. Bowie knew her students drew on their prior knowledge and her instruction, throughout several introductory lessons she critiqued the use of both visual and linguistic signs when viewing various web sites. These introductory lessons influenced the style of students' compositions.

While consuming and critiquing the configurations of various semiotic signs encountered on web pages, Mrs. Bowie adopted two terms, *kid-friendly text* and *adult-friendly text*. She used these lessons to construct and shape the students' definitions of kid-friendly and adult-friendly multimodal texts, and emphasized that the audience for this project was other fifth-grade students, hence the appropriate text style was a kid-friendly text.

Together Mrs. Bowie and the students critiqued the design elements (e.g., linguistic, visual, and audio) located on the web sites. The Environmental Protection Agency (www.epa.gov/acidrain/education/site_students/) had a web site that specifically addressed acid rain and included two links to both an adult site and student site. With audience in mind, Mrs. Bowie had the students read both sites. Then the following whole-group conversation occurred and began to shape how the different sign systems functioned in a kid-friendly text:

Mrs. Bowie: Who is your audience for your presentation?
April: Children.
John: Kids.
Abigail: Children.
Gabby: Fifth graders.
Mrs. Bowie: Kids. So which one looks more kid friendly?
April: The student site.
Unison Response: Student site.

Mrs. Bowie: So when you are planning your storyboard you want to keep that kind of stuff in mind. You want to think about who is your audience? Are they kindergarteners or fifth graders? They're fifth graders just so you all know. And what is going to make them attracted to your home page?
April: Fun, colors.
John: Colors.
Mrs. Bowie: Colors and animation.
April: Yeah.
Mrs. Bowie: Cartooney looking things look a lot better than technical things.

This discussion reveals several important points. First, Mrs. Bowie and the students identified the visual elements of colors, animations, and "cartooney" images as being kid friendly or less "technical." Mrs. Bowie and the students only identified types of visual elements on the screen and did not discuss how meaning was spread across the visual and linguistic elements on the page. Second, Mrs. Bowie also alluded to the idea that the students had to attract their audience so that they would read their multimodal compositions and color was one way to do that. Looking throughout the entire data set, I saw that Mrs. Bowie's repeatedly positioned the use of visual elements as a way to grab the reader's attention or serve as an aesthetic element (Dondis, 1973).

As the lesson continued, Mrs. Bowie and the children further defined the conventions for a kid-friendly text. In the excerpt below, notice the content of the exchange between Mrs. Bowie, April, and John, while viewing a web site together.

April: Oh, cool. [laughing]
Mrs. Bowie: Kid friendly or adult friendly?
John: Kid friendly.
Mrs. Bowie: What makes it so kid friendly?
John: Color, the skull. [image of a skull and cross bones was on the page]

Previously, Mrs. Bowie and the children had identified color as one visual element that created kid-friendly text. This conversation expanded the visual design structure to explore specific cultural images, the skull and crossbones, along with color. The specific example presented above stands in contrast to the very general references to "cartooney" images in the previous excerpt.

During another point of the whole class lesson, Mrs. Bowie switched web sites and talked about ways the students could add color through Word Art. As Mrs. Bowie talked, April saw an animation of a lemon-shaped face making sour facial expressions come up on the enlarged screen. She had an immediate affective response to the animation:

April: [laughing loudly] Look at the picture! [laughing again]
Mrs. Bowie: And even look at the font. It is a fun reading font, not that technical stuff. So kid friendly. This is pretty much all that there is. [referring to lack of written text and reading the title] "What is Acid Rain?" Look at the graphics they are using just to get you going.
April: A lemon. [laughing]
Mrs. Bowie: Gives you some examples. You're liking the looks of it without even reading it. Obviously kid friendly.
April: Oh, YEAH!

A close interpretation of this exchange provides insight into the combination of two semiotic design elements, visual and linguistic. Consistent with the earlier excerpts, the importance of affectively grabbing the reader's attention through the use of "graphics they are using just to get you going" is apparent through both April's and Mrs. Bowie's comments on the visual appeal of the site. Mrs. Bowie's comment, "You like the looks of it without even reading it" reflects the belief that the visuals served an affective purpose, which differs from the reading of print (e.g., information), a cognitive purpose.

Here, we see Mrs. Bowie position the use of design elements for use in specific, but limited ways. Referring to the design elements in this way is important because it portrays a view that written words represent important information while visual images are used for aesthetic purposes or to complement the linguistic elements. This emphasis on aesthetic uses of visual images limits the potential affordances of that mode (Kress, 1998), and more specifically overlooks the notion that visual images can act as tools for meaning making just as they can act as tools for aesthetic purposes (McVee, Bailey, Shanahan, 2008). Kress argues that layering modes and meaning can result in effective, powerful communication. In the next section, I turn to the impact of presenting the visual and linguistic sign systems in this way by showing how it shaped the students' multimodal text compositions.

Designing: Students' Use of Signs

After Mrs. Bowie and the students discussed the expectations of the assignment, students began to compose their own HyperStudio multimodal texts from their various scientific perspectives. During this time Mrs. Bowie and the students typically went to the library and worked at the bank of computers. Students moved between collaboration at the tables to composing at the computers. While the students were constructing their own knowledge and deciding how to represent that knowledge using digital technologies, Mrs. Bowie moved throughout the library facilitating the process.

When students constructed their multimodal text they mainly focused their sign use in layouts on the screen in three different ways: (a) visual design elements, (b) linguistic design elements, or (c) a combination of visual and linguistic design elements with the printed word being the primary information medium and the visual design repeating some aspect of the printed word. Throughout this section, the layouts mentioned above and sign system uses are explored through the product (i.e., home card and story cards) and transcripts revealing students' discussion while in the act of composing.

Design of Home Card: Emphasis on the Visual Mode.

When the students designed their home card (i.e., first card of the stack) from a chemist's, biologist's, or economist's perspective, they primarily used visual design elements with the goal of introducing their perspective and grabbing the readers' attention. Figure 7.1 below serves as an example of a home card. Note that the title Danielle and Jeremy should have put on the top-center of the page was "economy" since their research perspective was an economist's perspective. The transcript of their discussion and text analyses revealed that both Jeremy and Danielle initially struggled with the vocabulary word "economist" and due to confusion titled the page "ecology" instead of "economy." When viewing the home card in Figure 7.1, focus on the signs Jeremy and Danielle choose to represent their economist view of acid rain's effect on the economy and the instruction.

Notice how Danielle and Jeremy mainly relied on visual design elements for their home card. The only places Danielle and Jeremy used the linguistic design elements on the home card were for the title of the card, "Ecology" and for the word "Home" below the icon of a house. All students limited their use

FIGURE 7.1 Danielle and Jeremy's card with a visual narrative layout

of linguistic designs to the title in large print at the top-center of the page and used the printed word again for the Home button for their home cards. This finding aligned with Mrs. Bowie's initial instruction where she emphasized that the use of visual signs would grab the readers' attention so the reader would be "brought places that teach you things, where the words are"

When analyzing the transcript and the multimodal composition together, Danielle and Jeremy's inability to communicate their intended message through the visual mode became apparent. Unfortunately, because Danielle and Jeremy focused primarily on the visual mode of communication, a great deal of their intended meaning was lost in their redesign of the acid rain content. For instance, when Danielle was sharing her home card with a peer, Danielle referred to her scene on her home card as one meant to depict a community affected by acid rain. In Danielle's discussion with Emily she said, "Do you like the fish? This is like a community and when all the acid rain falls it destroys this community. This is like an environment that gets destroyed." As Danielle talked, she traced her finger in a circular motion on the screen to show all the salient elements and their interrelatedness in the environment. She further discussed the ill effects of acid rain with Emily.

Danielle: The community will suffer because of the acid rain. See this is a bank over here [where she is pointing], and they will need billions of dollars to fix the damages. These fish [pointing to the fish in the water] will die because they are swimming in acid rain.

Emily: Ohh! That's sad! Poor fishy!

Danielle: See the car? [pointing to the car on the bridge] It will rust and the paint will chip off. Oh, yeah the buildings will crack and the bridge too.

Through Danielle's conversation it was evident that she had a great deal of knowledge about the economic consequences of acid rain on land, and man-made objects such as cars, buildings and bridges. By choosing to use mainly visual design elements seen in Figure 7.1, Danielle, as well as the other groups, put the reader at a disadvantage. Focusing primarily on one sign system and not knowing the affordances and limitations of sign systems resulted in the multimodal text not providing enough information for the reader to interpret all that Danielle had intended to signify. For example, it was unlikely that a reader would interpret the significance of the dollar sign in the corner means that acid rain costs the community a great deal of money.

Furthermore, in a different conversation with Jeremy, Danielle indicated the gray object on the left side of the screen was a bank. The roughly drawn bank was not recognizable as a bank because it had no linguistic label. Additionally, Danielle knew that bridges, buildings, and the car would deteriorate due to acid rain and intended to convey that meaning through their visual display. However, without having access to the conversation that occurred while the students composed the multimodal composition, most readers, including the teacher, would not be able to access the depth of information about acid rain that Danielle possessed. Kress (1998) comments that one of the capacities of visual modes of communication is to display information for the reader and one of the capacities of the linguistic mode is to orient the reader to the information being conveyed through visual signs. In this case, Danielle did not understand all the capabilities of the visual and linguistic design elements, resulting in a less complex message being conveyed to her reader.

In this situation, by spreading meaning across modes, Danielle could have conveyed a clearer message by orienting the reader to the information that she visually displayed. For example, even if Danielle wanted to leave her display as primarily visual she could have recorded her voice adding the information through speech as opposed to losing part of her visual design by adding a block of writing. Spreading meaning across multiple modes can create a more coherent multimodal text and a more comprehensive representation of content knowledge. Not discussing the interrelatedness and interdependence between design elements was common for the students in this class. Within this classroom context, Mrs. Bowie and the students never asked, "What is afforded by combining these modes?"

Design of Story Cards: Emphasis on the Visual and Linguistic Signs

Unlike the home card that primarily drew upon visual design elements, the linked story cards used primarily linguistic signs. When visual signs were used, they were used to complement—not extend—the meaning of the linguistic signs. Thus, Danielle and Jeremy's layout in Figure 7.2 represented the

FIGURE 7.2 Jeremy and Danielle's card—visiual design complements linguistic design

way most of the groups designed their story cards. In the excerpt below, they attempted to figure out how to incorporate visual design elements on the page to represent particular concepts such as "economy." Through viewing the story card and the transcript of the conversation that occurred as Jeremy and Danielle composed the story card, it was clear they questioned how visual and linguistic signs function together in the multimodal composition within the classroom context.

Danielle: Ok, now, Economy, if we want to write about buildings we should draw buildings. Right? We can make a building right over here.
Jeremy: Make a building and then put cracks on it.
Danielle: I don't know if we'll find a picture that has a building with cracks in it, ok.
Jeremy: Then we'll find a picture of a dollar bill. Mrs. Bowie?
Mrs. Bowie: Yes
Jeremy: For our pictures and stuff, and this card is suppose to be how it affected buildings and stuff. Can we just have a building and then how it affects money, put a dollar bill?
Mrs. Bowie: Whatever works to tell the story? I don't mind.

Danielle's first comment demonstrated her interpretation and knowledge of the function of sign systems on story cards within the context of this fifth-grade class: images function to repeat or reflect the information stated through the linguistic design elements. She said, "If we want to write about a building, we should draw a building. Right?" Further, Danielle revealed her ability to think about sign system use when she questioned, "Right?" Jeremy and Danielle further checked their understanding by asking Mrs. Bowie about how to use the picture. Danielle and Jeremy's conventional use of visual and linguistic modes was very typical in school and thus commonplace for the students.

A Glimpse at Layering

Up to this point, all of the examples I have presented have been representative of all participants. However, there was one story card in the data set that was a discrepant case and revealed more complex use of sign systems. I present this discrepant case because it revealed what could result if students within the school context considered the capabilities of the various modes and how to spread meaning across the modes. One story card, designed by John and Abigail, represented synchronous use of both the visual and linguistic design elements where the design elements were interrelated and relied on one another to communicate a more complete and complex message. Their multimodal composition and discourse from the transcript unveiled a more complex interplay between design elements.

FIGURE 7.3 John and Abigail's card—more synchronous use of visual and linguistic design elements.

In Figure 7.3, the incorporation of the writing blocks in a circular pattern joined with arrows tied the salient visual and linguistic design elements together. Without the linguistic text, the reader would not understand the cyclical nature of acid rain and how acid rain impacted the entire ecosystem. Using the cyclical pattern that included arrows with the linguistic text allowed the reader to see the complex interconnected relationship that existed within the environment. Exclusively using the visual design elements, or exclusively using the linguistic design elements in a linear bulleted format, would not have communicated such an engaging and informational message about the interactive relationship acid rain has in our ecosystem.

In Figure 7.3, John and Abigail attempted to describe what occurred within the environment when acid rain was present and the discourse from the transcripts revealed how form and meaning were combined (Kress, 2003) as they planned their page.

John: It's like water, land, water, apples, land.
Abigail: Land over here, water here. Should I have it like this? [meaning water on one side, land on the other side of the screen] They are all affecting each other.
John *With the cycle. What do you think of this idea?*
Abigail: A cycle! You are saying trees around the acidic lake die?
John: That's part of the conflict.
Abigail: This is how acidic water systems affect us.

Notice Abigail began with a split screen revealing land on one side and water on the other. However, Abigail questioned the split screen layout because as she indicated, "they are all affecting each other." This self-questioning indicated that Abigail was evaluating her ability to convey and represent her intended message. Through collaboration with John, Abigail added the "cycle" design to represent an ecosystem's interrelated relationship. When presenting this card to their peers, they stated, "The cycle keeps going on until you have a dead ecosystem." Because Abigail and John spread meaning across linguistic and visual design elements their message was more clearly conveyed than in some of the other cards.

Unlike the previous examples, Figure 7.3 and the transcripts show Abigail moving back and forth between design elements and her understanding of the impact of acid rain. When representing her knowledge Abigail attended to the intricacies of her understanding of acid rain in the ecosystem, when moving from one sign system to the next. Abigail appeared to rely on her own knowledge about multimodal composing that did not parallel what she had been taught in school. In the next section, I discuss how the students rarely used audio signs to represent meaning, instead they used audio signs to elicit an affective response.

Auditory Design Elements

In the multimodal compositions, students had the ability and opportunity to spread meaning through the use of transition sounds. The data set revealed only one group of students discussed the use of transition sounds while composing their multimodal compositions. Upon viewing the finished products across the entire class, it became evident that the students selected the sounds that they liked and did not focus on how the transition sound could represent the content or convey the message. For example, the chemistry partners used an elephant sound as a transition between the following two cards (see Figures 7.4 and 7.5).

The elephant sound did not relate to either the home card titled "chemistry" or the story card presenting two chemicals that make up acid rain, sulfer dioxide or nitrogen dioxide. April and Krystal never asked, "What could sound do for the message of my multimodal composition?" Approaching the use of audio signs, as forms of communication used to convey meaning, instead of simple tools on a software program might have resulted in students composing a more comprehensive and complex multimodal text.

What We Learn from Mrs. Bowie and Her Students

Mrs. Bowie's efforts to include multimodal literacies into her existing curriculum were laudable. The fact that she was willing to take a risk to accept that she could learn from the students was crucial to the technology integration.

FIGURE 7.4 Home card, chemistry

However, due to her the professional development being focused on "how to" use digital technologies her background knowledge was limited in how to represent meaning with visual, audio, and linguistic signs.

In this study Mrs. Bowie's positioning of sign use, and the social, historical context within the school shaped how students constructed their multimodal text and constrained their use of various sign systems to communicate effectively. As we have seen, having the tools within the software program is not

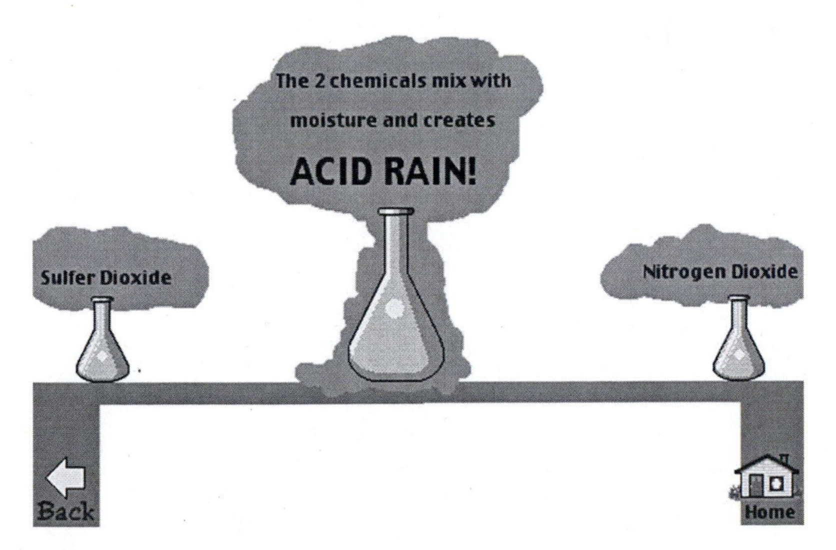

FIGURE 7.5 Sound linked chemistry card

enough; students and teachers must understand the potentials of communicating multimodally. Central to moving beyond writing as print-based is the direct attention in professional development to the orchestration of multiple modes of communication.

To assist educators and students in meeting the challenges of writing multimodal text, teachers need to learn the affordances and limitations of various sign systems. Also attending to the layering of meaning between sign systems becomes most critical. Because Mrs. Bowie and the students positioned the use of linguistic signs to convey information and visual signs to gain the readers attention, they missed the opportunity to use the all three design elements in conjunction with one another. Not one story card integrated all three—visual, linguistic, and auditory—design elements to create a comprehensive message. I argue that a talented teacher, such as Mrs. Bowie, should have the opportunity to learn about the affordances and limitations of various signs. Then, armed with this knowledge, she could better facilitate students' understandings of how to compose a comprehensive multimodal text such as the one Abigail and John began constructing in Figure 7.3.

In thinking about implications for instruction, there are number of questions that Mrs. Bowie, other teachers, and students can ask themselves as they engage in the design process:

1. What can the design elements—visual, linguistic, or audio—do to convey my message?
2. What are the limitations in using the various design elements to communicate my message?
3. How can I combine the use of the design elements to spread the meaning across the modes when attempting to convey my message?
4. How does the use of various design elements deepen meaning and presentation of knowledge?

These four questions might serve as a catalyst for shifting the focus from relying on linguistic signs only for meaning, to combining all modes—visual, auditory, gestural, and linguistic—as the synergy for making meaning. This shift in focus, however, remains a challenge for educators.

Additionally, these findings argue for expanding the definition of writing to include the writing of and with multiple sign systems. Through examining Mrs. Bowie's instruction, it was evident that potential uses of various sign systems were influenced by the material and social, cultural histories (Jewitt & Kress, 2003) of sign use within the school context. This change in definition assumes a multimodal semiotic approach to reading and writing where visual, linguistic, audio, and gestural design elements can be essential information mediums that engage readers cognitively and aesthetically.

References

Dondis, D. A. (1973). *A primer of visual literacy.* Cambridge, MA: MIT Press.

Gee, J. P. (1991). A linguistic approach to narrative. *Journal of Narrative Life History, 1,* 15–39.

Gee, J. P. (1996). *Social linguistics and literacies.* New York: Routledge.

International Reading Association. (2009). *Integrating technology in the curriculum: A position statement.* Retrieved from http://www.reading.org/positions/technology.html

Jewitt, C., & Kress, G. (2003). *Multimodal literacy.* New York: Peter Lang.

Kress, G. (1998). Visual and verbal modes of representation in electronically mediated communication: the potentials of new forms of text. In I. Snyder (Ed.), *Page to screen taking literacy into the electronic era* (pp. 5–79). London: Routledge.

Kress, G. (2003). *Literacy in the new media age.* London: Routledge.

MacArthur, C. A. (2006). The effects of new technologies on writing and writing processes. In C. A. MacArthur, S. Graham, & J. Fitzgerald (Eds.), *Handbook of writing research* (pp. 208–221). New York: Guilford Press.

McVee, M. B., Bailey, N M., & Shanahan, L. E. (2008). Using digital media to interpret poetry: Spiderman meets Walt Whitman. *Research in Teaching of English, 43*(2), 112–143.

New London Group (1996). A pedagogy of multiliteracies: Designing social futures. *Harvard Educational Review, 66*(1), 60–92.

8

A LITERACY PEDAGOGY FOR MULTIMODAL COMPOSING

Transforming Learning and Teaching

Suzanne M. Miller, Mary K. Thompson, Ann Marie Lauricella, and Fenice B. Boyd, with Mary B. McVee

Nicole: Who was Jim Crow? Why did he get to make laws?
Paige: I don't think he was a real person, I think that the name came because a crow is black and the laws were for black people.
Nicole: Then where did Jim come from?
Paige: I don't know.

In their class, 16-year-olds Nicole and Paige then moved immediately to the classroom computer to find answers to their questions. In a few minutes, they located some clues from a search engine and were off on an inquiry into multimodal texts (e.g., Library of Congress newspaper accounts and advertisements from the time, photographs, literacy tests, political cartoons). They pitched their plan to their teacher, who offered suggestions and gave permission for using music instead of narrative in some parts. Using historical skills to "read" these texts, they designed a story as a digital video in the genre of a movie trailer: it was set to the music of Billie Holiday singing the haunting words of "Strange Fruit," as graphic images flashed across the screen. They also drew on vernacular history from their community about what they knew about the Jim Crow era and enacted scenes about segregation, using the school water fountain bearing the sign, "Whites Only." From here, Paige and Nicole composed what was to become a startling digital video on discrimination and lynching in the post-Civil War era in the United States. Much as with professional filmmakers, their two-minute production took hours of research, corroboration of evidence through sourcing, conversation, takes and re-takes, and editing to integrate audio and visual modes. Their work culminated in a stunned classroom of urban teens moved by the "premiere" of *For Colored Only*—the eventual title of their movie that was "coming soon to a theatre near you." In the end, they composed not just an understanding of the origin of Jim Crow and Jim Crow laws, but an orchestration of multimodal texts engaging the auditory and visual senses, and presenting a deep, critical understanding of lynching as a horrific event in America's history (adapted from Lauricella, 2007, see also 2006).

A Story of Change through Multimodal Composing

In this classroom vignette, Nicole and Paige integrated their strategies for historical thinking and evaluation of sources learned in school with their strategies learned out of school for answering questions. They looked into their history textbook, sought valid information from their communities, and searched archives on the Internet. Reading an original newspaper advertisement for a lynching online stunned them—these were not spontaneous events. Seeing photographs of proud perpetrators sickened them (http://www.americanlynching.com/pic1.htm); contemplating a photograph of a man "saved" from lynching led to questions about how people could live with such emotional trauma; and hearing the stark haunting tones of Billie Holiday's song shocked them into understanding the horror of who was hanging from the bloody trees. [To view their video, go to http://gse.buffalo.edu/org/cityvoices/festmov/featured.php.]

What made Paige and Nicole's in-school inquiry for digital composing possible? We argue here that it was a convergence of conditions that worked to reframe what could happen in school. It's important to consider that Nicole and Paige and their millennial classmates come to school with new literacies (new kinds of texts and uses of texts in their lives), which too often they are required to leave at the classroom door—like guns in the old West (Gee, 2004). Among many others, Cope and Kalantzis (2000) recommend drawing on these new literacies in school through immersion in experiences with designing meaning that make "intuitive sense" to learners because they appear in realms outside of school (p. 244).

Digital video composing, for example, is a high-status social and cultural practice with powerful attention-getting qualities and expert versions in the real world (e.g., Miller, 2007). The connection to youth-media culture (music videos, YouTube, vlogs) is strong, making it a high-interest endeavor that draws on student out-of-school knowledge. Understanding implicitly the purpose and structure of movie trailers as a media genre is part of youth culture—as evidenced by the numerous websites devoted just to these video texts. Use of this familiar media genre in DV composing created a school connection to the media sphere (e.g., Burgess & Green, 2009).

Further, Nicole and Paige's innovative teacher Keith Hughes (an active participant in the Buffalo Digital Video Composing Project[1]) provided them with the opportunity to compose a digital video movie trailer as a tool for understanding the Jim Crow era in America; their intense interest in pursuing the questions they had raised and composing/publishing their own movie trailer led them to examine not only print texts but also other modes for understanding—images, music, enacted movement, narratives. In the vignette at the beginning of the chapter, these available *multimodal* resources and the girls' orchestration of them, supported at points of need by their teacher, brought lived historical experience to the classroom and to their concentrated attention. "Doing history" requires the ability to analyze and read documents, which Paige and Nicole learned in the process of doing, moving beyond the collection of facts to tell a story. They "read" and sourced and analyzed the documents (Wineburg, 2001) and learned that "facts" changed depending on who was telling the story.

Why Multimodal Inquiry?

This story of an innovative classroom is not like most classrooms, though. In contrast, some schools have been focused only on print texts for many years and have been slow to change. Critiques of traditional schooling point to the "more compelling and motivating" multimodal learning that students engage in outside of school (Gee, 2004; Kalantzis & Cope, 2008) to explain the increasing student disengagement in classrooms. Although students outside of school use computers and cell phones (and other ubiquitous computing devices) to remain almost continuously linked to resources, people, and networks for information and communication, these phenomena have often been treated as separate, private and non-school-like. We believe many students desperately want to see school as connected to who they are and are becoming, but a striking majority of even the most successful students today feel that school is devoid of connection to their "real life" (Lenhart, Madden, & Hitlin, 2005). In the DV Composing project, we have found that teacher engagement with the multimodal and digital lives of students can provide for curricular connections to their emerging new literacies and create new opportunities for teaching and learning (Miller, 2007, 2008a).

The digital explosion we are now experiencing has created a world in which such educational changes are more critical than ever before. New Literacy scholars have become categorical in their conclusions: "In the modern world, print literacy is not enough" (Gee, 2003, p. 19). Facility with interpreting and designing *multimodal texts* will increasingly be required by human beings to communicate, work, and thrive in the digital, global world of the 21st century. Many scholars agree, also, that important changes will be needed in schooling, in teachers, and, especially, in educational beliefs about the status/design of non-print modes as ways of understanding knowledge and representing meaning (e.g., Gee & Hayes, 2011). Those changes, we have found, can prompt transformations in student learning.

For instance, Paige and Nicole described how their video had a deep impact on their understanding. A week after they screened their *For Colored Only* video for the class, Nicole and Paige encountered a school fight brewing over someone stepping on a friend's white sneakers. In an instant, they brought their new knowledge of history to their lives, intervening to stop the fight. Nicole later explained, "Why would they fight about such a stupid thing? After everything that was fought for, why fight over this?" (Lauricella, 2006, p. 140). Paige continued the story: "But I think after our movie, look what they [African Americans and some Whites] had to go through. You're arguing because your boyfriend looked at me, because your sneakers are dirty? You know? Is it that serious?" (Lauricella, 2006, pp. 140–141). Through their joint efforts, based on their new and deep understanding of their social-historical context, Paige and Nicole stopped this cafeteria fight. Their passionate grasp of their in-school inquiry led them to read their world critically and historically and, then, take action to transform it.

If educators value such deep knowledge and learning in schools (and we do), what can we do to help it happen? In our work in the New Literacies Group at the University at Buffalo, a major goal is understanding how best to help pre-service and in-service teachers in our classes to take into account their students' lifeworlds (i.e., worldviews from lived experiences) (Holland, Lachiocotte, Skinner, & Cain, 1998) *and* their social futures in the 21st century (New London Group, 1996). We are not so interested in "how to use X technology" in classrooms, but rather in how to engage teachers in rethinking what we do in English Language Arts (ELA) and other content-area classes. For us, the needed changes in what some call "New Times" (Luke & Elkins, 1998) are less technological and more epistemological: the critical issue is what counts as knowing and, therefore, what counts as learning and effective teaching?

Reframing Pedagogies

We believe that a fundamental shift is needed in the way we in education think about subject-matter content in order to create pedagogical opportunities that not only meet the standards of state-mandated exams, but also connect to the longing of students for classrooms that are interactive, inspiring, and connected to their lives and futures. Our key concern is how all of us (teachers and teacher educators) can draw on and help to shape student identities through multimodal literacy practices afforded by the digital world, in order to create productive civic, personal, and social futures for the early generations of the new century.

Influential thinking related to these issues and our own research findings suggest that what we call multimodal literacy pedagogy is a promising framework for 21st-century teaching and learning. By *multimodal literacy pedagogy* (MLP) we mean a reframing of teaching that connects the literacy identities and practices of our students through purposeful multimodal activities in supportive social spaces to potentially change classrooms and learning (also see

Boyd & Canteen, 2008; McVee, Bailey, & Shanahan, 2007, 2008a,b; Miller, 2007, 2008a,b,c, 2010a,b; Thompson, 2008).

From our sociocultural perspective, with an eye to the changes needed in traditional education, we believe a theory of pedagogical change is needed to integrate theoretical explanations with classroom practice in order to elaborate the role of purposeful, mediated multimodal activity in the complex dynamics of schools. The *design* of the pedagogy needs to be central *if* it is to guide teachers and teacher educators in creating 21st-century classrooms. We propose that our framework for a multimodal literacy pedagogy provides such an integrative theory for designing pedagogical change in a changing world.

Multimodal Literacy Pedagogy: Designing Transformative Classrooms

This pedagogical theory for multimodal teaching and learning integrates identity-making literacy practices with attention to purposeful multimodal design in order to reframe teaching for the 21st century. The principles that we have derived from our analysis of relevant theory and our own multimodal composing research in schools and teacher education classes identify the dynamics of multimodal pedagogy and explain the transformative nature of its defining ideologies, tools, materials, attitudes, beliefs, and values.

The following sections provide an overview of the central framework elements by drawing on the dynamics of the classroom in which the digital video *For Colored Only* was designed and produced by Paige and Nicole.

Creating Supported Social Spaces for Designing Texts

From the multimodal literacy pedagogy perspective, the notion of knowledge as only a propositional language product held by the teacher and transferred to individual students *changes to* the notion of knowledge as multimodal, *co-constructed*, and performed or represented, not absorbed (Lankshear & Knobel, 2003, 2006). For instance, Paige and Nicole's teacher, Keith Hughes, describes the social space he developed to provide the tools, resources, and opportunities that he felt students needed (Miller, Hughes, & Knips, in press):

> The physical set up is another variable that I can control in order to facilitate the students' experience. [Figure 8.1] is a visual representation of my physical classroom. This will become an important multimodal element in order to put into context many of the other methods I will be discussing, including digital video instruction ... as well as activities steeped more heavily in traditional modes of meaning such as reading and writing. Students pick up their work when they walk in and sit around what I like to call, the electric campfire. My lecture stand is set up with a Mac for LCD use with stereo sound. Thirteen aging Macintosh G3's grace the

> outskirts of the room [only 5 work dependably], leaving a comfortable amount of space for up to three students to be working on one computer. The first one-third of classroom when you enter is open, allowing for student filming and other classroom activities. In front of the room white space has become my digital blackboard with my trusted mini-mac sending its contents through the LCD. As students enter the room they are met with a five foot by five foot image of classroom messages.

This design represents Keith's pedagogical knowledge and principles for his multimodal literacy pedagogy. The space communicates his goals for routines (pick up handouts, read projected announcements) and innovation (spaces for group work at computers and in performance areas). In addition, the walls are completely covered with multimodal historical texts—e.g., depression photographs, political cartoons, and documents like the Bill of Rights—interspersed with startling things like a large Pinocchio puppet. The room is alive with tools, artifacts, and evocative objects (the prop box with a hodge-podge of items, including a graduation mortar board, a length of cotton, aluminum foil, lab coat, etc.) (see Pahl & Rowsell, 2010).

In this space Paige and Nicole conducted their multimodal inquiry. Their classroom social space permitted them to develop jointly a question important to them and then to take their inquiry to the Internet, where they were able to find relevant multimodal texts others had published there. They enlisted the social support of their teacher, other students (they prepped and paid the student enacting a scene of discrimination), and their relatives in the community (Nicole's mother suggested the "Strange Fruit" music). In their collaborative

FIGURE 8.1 A social space for composing understanding

team they discussed at length whether the lynching pictures were too "gruesome" or whether they were necessary to communicate the full outrage they wanted the audience to feel.

A sustaining impetus for these efforts was the ultimate publishing of their inquiry in a quintessential multimodal form—as a digital video screened for their classmates and published back to the web. Through the supportive classroom social space, then, they collaborated and felt themselves part of the network of knowledge production that the digital age affords. With support at points of need, they used digital and human resources to create a new multimodal text that represented their new knowledge and meanings co-constructed through historical inquiry.

Drawing on a social view of learning and instruction and our research, we have found that this mediation or support provided by others is a central necessity in multimodal literacy pedagogy. Out of school, online, and in-person conversation can supply support for engaging in multimodal activities in groups organized around a joint endeavor. In school, students and the facilitating teacher can provide support during the whole process of multimodal composing activities.

The supportive talk during multimodal activities allows teachers and students to create openness to perspectives and contributions from multiple participants. This talk also provides opportunities for making the discourse of participation in composing explicit and for collaborating on diverse strategies for making sense of the curriculum and the world.

Drawing on Identity Lifeworlds As Literacy Resources

People are aware of identities as sister, father, friend, but often we have not systematically taken into account our identities shaped by affinities for reality TV, rap music, fantasy films, personal blogs, *anime*, YouTube, or chess. For example, reality TV fans bring their knowledge of social group interactions (who should be voted off next) to their "reading" of shows, read other's opinions online—and share their own on blogs, on TV-related web sites, and around the water cooler or coffee shop.

These out-of-school identities contribute to teacher and student literacy practices and, thereby, can serve as resources for re-seeing what is possible in classrooms. Too often we leave these practices and identities outside the classroom, thinking that they are separate from what goes on in schools. This false dichotomy (in- and out-of-school literacies) assumes that what students bring into classrooms does not matter (e.g., Hull & Schultz, 2002). Instead, we aim to make the identity resources of our students and teachers and their lifeworld experiences central to planning for and engaging with various modes of textual representation (i.e., with multimodal texts). The lifeworld experiences of millennial students provide a worldview that is important for students to use as a lens to connect what they know to what they are learning.

Keith Hughes was the first of the CVCV teachers to propose using media genres students already knew well in composing videos. For example, he introduced the digital video "uncommercial" genre and the movie trailer genre. These media genres had three important benefits: (a) students had implicit knowledge of media culture and advertisement structure that they could draw on and make explicit; (b) the familiar purpose of the form was appropriated consciously to sell an *idea* (curricular concept) or *narrative* (curricular chronicle); and (c) publishing the DV on the web made it part of the emerging clip culture (YouTube appeared in 2005), connecting it to the high-status youth practice of remixing culture to communicate ideas. Keith's students have "sold" such concepts as the Elastic Clause to the U. S. Constitution and Senetox, a remedy from Seneca Falls for the injustices against women. An iSpeak contrasting the printed text-book interpretation with the realities of Hiroshima can be seen at http://www.youtube.com/watch?v=8lgUBka-nio.

Paige and Nicole knew about movie trailers from their lifeworld experiences and were able to connect this media genre knowledge to their inquiry into Jim Crow, a topic that they did not know. They knew about discrimination from their own experiences and from the vernacular history they learned from parents and others—and drew on this knowledge as the impetus for and content of their movie, including the "Whites Only" sign above the school water fountain. In searching for music, Nicole asked her mother who helped her remember the "perfect" song she had heard long before. In such endeavors, students' identities and lifeworlds present potentials for their active engagement and connection inside multimodal literacies pedagogy.

Constructing Felt Purpose for Embodied Learning

As in all literacies, those authentically engaged in multimodal literacies are driven by a genuinely felt purpose for their embodied learning. By embodied learning, we mean engaging in learning through all the senses and forms of representation to understand deeply the specific meanings and ideas situated in the experience, not just literal, linear, propositional ones (Gee, 2004).

The *purpose* for engaging in the actions and talk of embodied learning, we argue, is usually deeply connected to participants' sense of identity and felt need for meaningful activity. When the "purpose" for school activities is motivated only by compliance or avoidance of punitive measures (e.g., bad grades), the reflective engagement necessary for understanding is missing (e.g., Borowicz, 2005). Research in classrooms suggests that the guiding purpose constructed for multimodal literacy practices in school cannot be for low-level comprehension and recall, but in some way must be about creating multimodal meaning and representation to bring curriculum and youth culture/out-of-school literacies and experiences together (e.g., Miller & Borowicz, 2006; Miller, 2008a, 2010a).

To negotiate an authentic purpose in his classroom, Keith Hughes took on a new role—what he called the "Executive Producer": He would set the task, but left many choices for students; he required the production teams to pitch their ideas, but then let them go to work out details. He rotated around the room to monitor groups, but set up the space so students could perform, compose, and edit with support of each other. During class, Keith provided support to help mediate student work when they needed assistance beyond the group.

In the initial consultation with a high school student group, Keith typically would ask, "What do you want to show?" or "What's your idea?" Focusing on students' communicative intent was one way that he created a new classroom purpose and order. When groups faltered, he'd suggest, "Use your storyboard as your guide" and "Call me back when you're done with your narrative." After student groups pitched their DV ideas, he'd often prompt for detail—"How will you present the text visually?" (Miller et al., in press).

Paige and Nicole first felt the need to answer their generated question about Jim Crow (Who was he? Why did he get to make laws?) and, then, to communicate the shocking findings of their inquiry about the planned, accepted nature of brutal lynching. Keith created a consistent message that inquiring into this historical period to understand the context (e.g., of the progressive era or the milieu for pieces of literature) was "doing history" and the purpose for digital video composing (Lauricella, 2006). For students, the purposes for engaging in multimodal literacy practices in school seem to be connected to repositioning themselves as competent communicators with ideas, worth, intellect. The adolescents in our research all responded to contexts where they *felt* authentic purpose. For instance, Darrius, a student constructed as a "thug" in school, felt competent for the first time in the classroom when he purposefully created a DV response to a class novel on the theme of loyalty. He followed that by composing a spoken word hip-hop poem to accompany a moving video elegy for a friend and a cousin (Borowicz, 2005). Co-constructing a felt sense of purpose beyond compliance may be the leading activity we as teachers need to take on as we bring multimodal composing to our students (Miller, 2010a).

Focusing Explicit Attention to Meaningful Multimodal Design

The idea of multimodal design emphasizes the active, generative process of creating meaning through multiple modes of representation, and not something governed by static rules (New London Group, 1996). This concept focuses our attention to the process of orchestrating representational (multimodal) resources and their interconnection. Designing is vital for composing a text that can meet the communication demands of new and future multimodal environments. Research shows, however, that in education we tend to under-use the affordances (i.e., available resources for performing actions) of multimodality because of our unconscious print bias and suggests that direct attention to the orchestration of multiple modes—to designing—is a promising approach to this problem (e.g., Bailey, 2006, this volume; Miller, 2008a; Shanahan, 2006, this volume).

The broad idea of *designing* includes the use of all the resources we have available to make meaning, the process of acting on those resources, and the product that represents transformed meanings and remixed textualities (Cope & Kalantzis, 2000; Kress, 2010). These multimodal semiotic (meaning-making) resources include such things as *linguistic* ways of interacting across contexts; *visual* resources for interpreting an event or idea through images—beyond reading about it in a print-based text; *audio* means of understanding through music, voices, or sound effects; and *kinesthetic* means of understanding through movement and enacting bodily performances.

The concept of design helps us to understand the social practices of multimodal representations *made* by people to communicate messages in the new landscape of communication where print is not necessarily the main mode (e.g., Kress, 2000, 2010). From the MLP perspective, knowing becomes a collaborative social activity that requires abilities to communicate, find, assemble, use and imagine new ways of envisioning assemblages of knowledge.

Keith attended to design even as he introduced the movie trailer assignment. As he handed out a rubric explaining the requirements for the project, he reviewed the criteria for storyboard images or narrative text, live video, dramatic voiceover, music to fit the meaning, and a flow of meaning to hold the DV together. Next, he showed a professional movie trailer for a horror film. He asked the class to count the clips as it played, explaining that clips are different shots taken by the camera. Students counted 38 shots in the 60-second movie trailer, and he reviewed each shot on the screen, pointing out the effect of angle, lighting, close-ups. Next, he focused on the music used in the trailer, explaining that the genre of the music had to match the mood and genre of the movie.

While he moved around to support student groups, he'd shout advice from across the room, "Don't shoot into the light!" or closer-up he'd advise, "Angle the shot to get a different feel or concept." After teaching a student how to use movie software to repeat a clip, he'd tell the student, "Go show Bill how to do that, he needs to know." During editing, students would call him over to review some footage, and he sometimes suggested, "You might try slowing down that clip to show your meaning better." If activity stalled, he'd introduce a next step for reflection: "What kind of mood do you want for your music?" He constantly focused attention on designing multimodally to communicate meaning, by modeling multimodality. He morphed from one mode to another as he guided understanding (pointing to the various printed texts around the room to help with context); offered ideas about lighting and "capturing" a shot; and directly pointed to software functions to extrapolate meaning behind a shot (the Ken Burns effect or "snow" on a black and white period piece). Keith "moves and shifts" and effortlessly changed roles as he glided through his classroom directly working with the kids at their point of need.

Such explicit attention to design in multimodal composing allows more conscious layering of representational modes to create complex meanings. In Paige and Nicole's class, Mr. Hughes made clear to students that they had access to photographs from the National Archive (i.e., of lynching); non-copyrighted music databases online (freeplaymusic.com) and in the room; voices, images, and gestures created by themselves and their classmates; objects in the classroom; props they could create (the "Whites Only" sign) or bring (the kerchief their actress wore); school spaces, including a long hallway with a water fountain; and examples of the movie trailer genre.

During the active process of making meaning and connecting multimodal resources for purposeful literacy work, Keith asked Nicole and Paige to pitch their idea for the movie trailer to him, suggested that they enact scenes to illustrate day-to-day life, and asked for their rationale for deleting some of the required narrative they had written and substituting Billie Holiday's singing of "Strange Fruit"—thus requiring their explicit explanation of their multimodal design elements. When they talked to an African American classmate to persuade her to wear a do-rag when they filmed her drinking at a water fountain with the sign "Whites Only," they were explicitly designing the multimodal elements of their movie in response to explicit instruction and support for designing their message.

For Colored Only transformed the movie trailer genre into a moving representation of a curricular inquiry with much evidence of attention to multimodal design elements: quick cuts from journalistic images of discrimination juxtaposed with enacted student scenes in black and white, connected those times with our times in a startling way; the stark photographs of bodies hanging overlaid with the haunting lyrics, "strange fruit hanging from the poplar trees," produced a chilling effect.

Paige and Nicole's performance was not directed by fixed rules. They collaborated to orchestrate and connect multimodal resources to communicate a heart-felt meaning they wanted others to feel and see as significant. With their teacher's support, they carefully layered the modes of meaning; they designed a message with deep impact for themselves and their astounded classmates.

Additionally, the discourse inherent in interacting with the material and evidence gathering, helped the girls to design their iMovie. If the old adage "you don't know what you think until you have read what you have written" is applied to multimodal literacies construction, the girls didn't know what to make of the evidence they were gathering until they negotiated their iMovie scenes. They talked with invested stakeholders (mother, researcher, teacher, classmates) and acted (using various props, movements, stages), and shot scenes (lighting, symbolic shots, camera angle), and set the tone (music, dialogue). The visual editing of the video told the story. When they finished, the story represented what they meant, which evolved as they planned. As they thought about what to represent, ideas about history and life emerged. This process moves beyond learning content: it explores the process of thinking and moves to creation of understanding

Critical Reframing Leads to Transformative Teaching and Learning

The changes in literacy practices in the digital age have already transformed what students bring to school. By drawing on the components that make up multimodal literacies outside of schools to critically reframe what happens in schools, we teachers and teacher educators can change the landscape of learning and teaching to redesign classroom pedagogy for the 21st century. In all, such change involves the process of reflecting on and redesigning pedagogy so that it (a) creates a supportive social space for mediation, (b) consistently constructs felt purpose for embodied teaching and learning, (c) draws upon the identity and lifeworlds of both students and teachers, and (d) provides explicit attention to and instruction in multimodal design. These critical reframings of what happens in classrooms can transform what counts as teaching, learning, knowing, and understanding in schools.

Figure 8.2 visually represents these principles of multimodal literacy pedagogy and suggests their transformative potential—through the critical reframing of teachers/teacher educators and their students in classrooms.

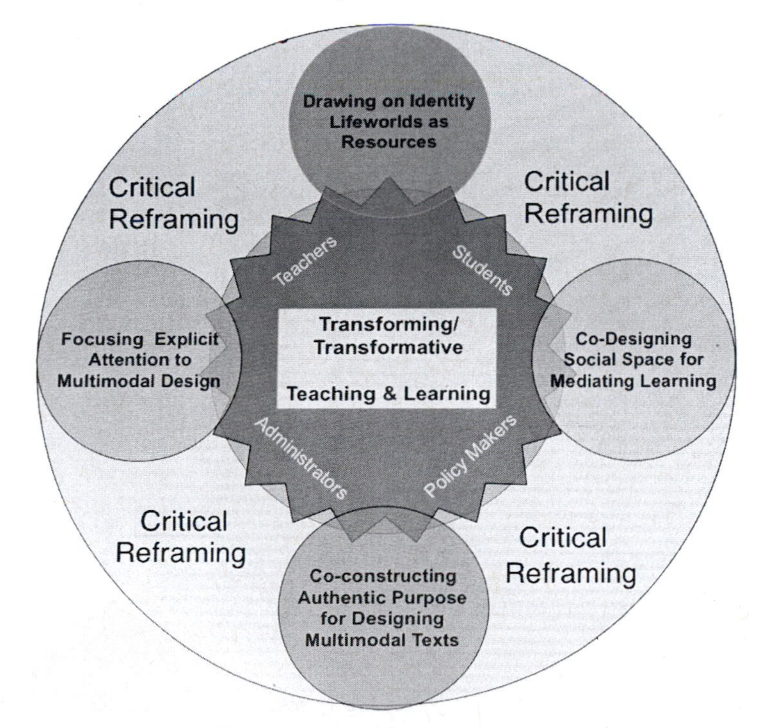

FIGURE 8.2 Multimodal literacy pedagogy: A framework for change

Of course, broader possibilities for change can occur when administrators in schools and policy makers in government also re-envision literacy and learning—a move visible in some policy reform documents (e.g., Partnership for 21st Century Skills, 2006; SCANS, 1999) and calls from professional organizations (e.g., National Council of Teachers of English, 2005, 2008; International Reading Association, 2001).

Integrating multimodal literacy pedagogy as a model for 21st-century learning in classrooms requires both teachers and students to take a reflective stance, stepping back to become aware of how design choices in supported social groups allow identity lifeworlds into schools and generate felt purposes for using multimodal resources to think, understand, and communicate in a digital world. Exploring why and how designing assemblages of images, sounds, music, and movements transform people and meanings is the central activity needed to broaden what we mean by literacy and to transform teaching and learning.

To contribute to this critical reframing of pedagogies, we as educators must attend to the identities of students, to critically consider how students' lifeworlds shape meaning-making and can re-shape literacy as meaningful in schools—as it did for Nicole and Paige. The ultimate goal of the proposed critical reframing through MLP is to move towards a transformative pedagogy—that is, 21st-century teaching that can critically transform millennial adolescent learners and their social futures in a digital world.

Going back once more to our introductory vignette, we see evidence that Keith Hughes reframed the classroom space and his teaching by providing Paige and Nicole the support and opportunity to re-see the world through an historical lens. We believe Keith's success emerged from his redesign of the classroom space to provide opportunity for the purposeful literacy practice of multimodal inquiry and digital video composing that for Paige and Nicole—and other students—changed the way they saw their everyday experience (see also Miller et al., in press). Narrative case studies of teachers and students working collaboratively to compose digitally in English and social studies classes provide other portraits of how student lifeworlds and identities can be connected to the curriculum through authentic multimodal literacy practices inside the classroom (e.g., Blondell, 2009; Borowicz, 2005; Cercone, 2009, 2010; Costello, 2006; Lauricella, 2006).

Finally, the use of MLP to describe the dynamics of multimodal composing can provide an explanation of how embodied experiences provide authentic purposeful literacies that teachers can draw on to reframe and transform their teaching (Boyd & Canteen, 2008; McVee et al., 2008a,b; Miller, 2007, 2008a,b,c; Thompson, 2008). It is our goal to make multimodal literacy pedagogy an urgent priority for educators. The principles of MLP can transform classrooms, and, we believe, can bridge the artificial gap between in- and out-of-school literacies and identities. It can change the teaching and teacher education landscape toward social design practices for felt purposes—the kind of civic, personal, and workplace futures envisioned by scholars and business and government leaders (e.g., Partnership for 21st Century Skills, 2006; Gee & Hayes, 2011; Kalantzis & Cope, 2008; Miller, 2008a; SCANS, 1991). By drawing on this MLP framework, we can re-envision our schools to be exemplary spaces for authentic learning of the kind Paige and Nicole experienced. Through the lens of MLP, we invite teachers and teacher educators to consider the possibilities for what our schools can become.

Note

1. City Voices, City Visions (CVCV) was a partnership between the University at Buffalo Graduate School of Education and the Buffalo Public Schools (BPS). Over 260 urban teachers have participated in CVCV professional development institutes aimed at preparing subject-area teachers to use DV composing as a new multimodal literacies tool for their 6th- to 12th-grade urban students. See www.CityVoicesCityVisions.org for more information.

References

Bailey, N. (2006). *Designing social futures: Adolescent literacy in and for new times*. Unpublished doctoral dissertation, University at Buffalo, State University of New York.

Blondell, M. (2009, April). *A teacher's design for digital video in English classrooms: Student learning in an urban high school*. Paper presented at the Annual Conference of the American Educational Research Association (AERA). San Diego.

Borowicz, S. (2005). *Embracing lives through the video lens: An exploration of literacy teaching and learning with digital video technology in an urban secondary English classroom*. Unpublished doctoral dissertation, University at Buffalo, State University of New York.

Boyd, F. B., & Canteen, C. (2008, March). *Learning multimodality: Digital immigrant goes digital native*. Presented at the Annual Conference of the American Educational Research Association (AERA), Chicago, IL.

Burgess, J., & Green, J. (2009). *YouTube*. Cambridge, UK: Polity Press.

Cercone, J. (2009, April). *The New Literacies classroom: Digital video composing in high school English*. Paper presented at the Annual Conference of the American Educational Research Association (AERA). San Diego.

Cercone, J. (2010). *Learning English in New Times: The Participatory design spaces of the new literacies classroom*. Unpublished doctoral dissertation, University at Buffalo, State University of New York.

Cope, B., & Kalantzis, M. (2000). Multiliteracies: The beginning of an idea. In B. Cope & M. Kalantzis (Eds.), *Multiliteracies: Literacy learning and the design of social futures* (pp. 3–8). London: Routledge.

Costello, A. (2006). *Digital video and drama production as literacy learning tools in English classrooms*. Unpublished doctoral dissertation, University at Buffalo, State University of New York.

Gee, J. (2003). *What video games have to teach us about learning and literacy*. New York: Palgrave Macmillan.

Gee, J. P. (2004). *Situated language and learning: A critique of traditional schooling*. New York: Routledge.

Gee, J. P., & Hayes, E. (2011). *Language and learning in the digital age*. New York: Routledge.

Holland, D. Lachiocotte, W. Skinner, D., & Cain, C. (1998). *Identity and agency in cultural worlds*. Cambridge, MA: Harvard University Press.

Hull, G., & Schultz, K. (Eds.). (2002). *School's out! Bridging out-of-school literacies with classroom pedagogy*. New York: Teachers College Press.

International Reading Association. (2001). *Integrating literacy and technology in the curriculum: A position statement.* Retrieved from http://www.reading.org/resources/issues/positions_technology.html

Kalantzis, M., & Cope, B. (2008). *New learning: Elements of a science of education.* London: Cambridge University Press.

Kress, G. (2000). Multimodality. In B. Cope & M. Kalantzis (Eds.), *Multiliteracies: Literacy learning and the design of social futures* (pp. 182–202). London: Routledge.

Kress, G. (2010). *Multimodality: A social semiotic view of contemporary communication.* New York: Routledge.

Lankshear, C., & Knobel, M. (2003). *New Literacies: Changing knowledge and classroom learning.* Philadelphia: Open University Press.

Lankshear, C., & Knobel, M. (2006). *New literacies: Everyday practices and classroom learning.* Philadelphia: Open University Press.

Lauricella, A. M. (2006). *Digital video production as a tool for learning: Exploring multiple text documents in an urban social studies classroom.* Unpublished doctoral dissertation, University at Buffalo, State University of New York.

Lauricella, A. M. (2007, April). *Digital video composing as an inquiry tool in the social studies classroom.* Paper presented at the Annual Conference of the American Educational Research Association (AERA), Chicago.

Lenhart, A., Madden, M., & Hitlin, P. (July, 2005). *Youth are leading the transition to a fully wired and mobile nation.* Washington, DC: Pew Internet & American Life Project.

Luke, A., & Elkins, J. (1998). Reinventing literacy in "New Times." *Journal of Adolescent & Adult Literacy, 42,* 4–7.

McVee, M. B., Bailey, N. M., & Shanahan, L. E. (2007, April). *Teachers first: Doing multimodality in literacy teacher education.* Paper presented at the American Educational Research Association (AERA), Chicago, IL.

McVee, M. B., Bailey, N. M., & Shanahan, L. E. (2008a). Using digital media to interpret poetry: Spiderman meets Walt Whitman. *Research in the Teaching of English, 43*(2), 112–143.

McVee, M. B., Bailey, N. M., & Shanahan, L. E. (2008b). Teachers and teacher educators learning from new literacies and new technologies. *Teaching Education, 19*(3), 197–210.

Miller, S. M. (2007, October). English teacher learning for new times: Digital video composing as multimodal literacy pedagogy. *English Education, 40*(1), 64–83.

Miller, S. M. (2008a). Teacher learning for new times: Repurposing new *multimodal* literacies and digital video composing for schools. In J. Flood, S. B. Heath, & D. Lapp (Eds.), *Handbook of research on teaching literacy through the communicative and visual arts* (Vol 2, 441–460). New York: International Reading Association/Simon & Schuster Macmillan.

Miller, S. M. (2008b, March). *Towards a multimodal literacy pedagogy: Digital video composing as teacher and student learning tool.* Paper presented at the Annual Conference of the American Educational Research Association (AERA), New York City.

Miller, S. M. (2008c, November). *Why multimodal literacies?* Presentation given at the CEE Awards Session at the National Council of Teachers of English Annual Conference, San Antonio, Texas.

Miller, S. M. (2010a). Reframing multimodal composing for student learning: Lessons on *Purpose* from the Buffalo DV project. *Contemporary Issues in Technology And Teacher Education, 10*(2). Retrieved from http://www.citejournal.org/vol10/iss2/maintoc.cfm

Miller, S. M. (2010b). Towards a multimodal literacy pedagogy: Digital video composing as 21st century literacy. In P. Albers (Ed.), *Becoming multimodal: 21st century literacy and the arts* (pp. 245–281). Urbana-Champaign: IL: National Council of Teachers of English.

Miller, S. M., & Borowicz, S. (2006). *Why multimodal literacies? Designing digital bridges to 21st century teaching and learning.* Buffalo, NY: GSE Publications.

Miller, S. M., Hughes, K., & Knips, M. (In press). Teacher knowledge-in-action: Digital video composing as 21st century literacy. In S. Kadjer & C. Young (Eds.), *Teaching English with technology.* Charlotte, NC: Academic Information Press.

New London Group. (1996). A pedagogy of multiliteracies: Designing social futures. *Harvard Educational Review, 66*, 60–92.

National Council of Teachers of English. (2005). *NCTE position statement: On multimodal literacies.* Retrieved from http://www.ncte.org/positions/statements/multimodalliteracies

National Council of Teachers of English. (2008). *NCTE position statement: Definition of 21st century literacies.* Retrieved from http://www.ncte.org/positions/statements/21stcentdefinition

Partnership for 21st Century Skills (2006). *Results that matter: 21st century skills and high school reform.* Retrieved from http://www.21stcenturyskills.org/documents/RTM2006.pdf

Pahl, J., & Rowsell, J. (2010). *Artifactual literacies: Every object tells a story.* New York: Teachers College Press.

Shanahan, L. E. (2006). *Reading and writing multimodal texts through information and communication technologies.* Unpublished doctoral dissertation, University at Buffalo, State University of New York.

The Secretary's Commission on Achieving Necessary Skills (SCANS) (1999). *Skills and Tasks for Jobs: A SCANS report for America 2000.* Washington, DC: U.S. Department of labor. Retrieved from http://wdr.doleta.gov/opr/fulltext/document.cfm?docn=6140

Thompson, M. K. (2008, March). *Multimodal pedagogy: Learning to develop content literacies for millennial youth.* Paper presented at the annual conference of the American Educational Research Association (AERA). New York.

Wineburg, S. (2001). *Historical thinking and other unnatural acts: Charting the future of teaching the past.* Philadelphia: Temple University Press.

9

CHANGING THE GAME

Teaching for Embodied Learning through Multimodal Composing

Suzanne M. Miller and Mary B. McVee

Tensions, Triumphs, and Subversive Activity

The classrooms described in these chapters are filled with activity and action. We were struck again and again across the stories by the movement within the classroom: the sense of embodied encounters, kids changing and moving and talking, kids looking at video on computers, kids acting out scenes, teachers circulating the room, a touch here, a question there, a video viewing here, a written draft reading there. This physical movement seems representative of the dynamics of a multi-person reality game and teachers not really knowing where they will end up and pretty consistently (it seems) being somewhat surprised, fulfilled, and pleased—"Hey, we made that!" "Hey, I taught that!" "Hey, my kids created this!" There is little that is passive and receptive in these rooms. In these classrooms, participants were agents of their own learning, going somewhere new together.

Tensions With Old-Yet-Present Ghosts

Yet Fordism, the antiquated philosophy of education as the transmission of knowledge to passive learners along an assembly line (e.g., Kalantzis & Cope, 2008), still haunts today's schools. Tensions in classrooms and in teachers can be traced to this wrong-headed idea that knowledge, fully formed, is delivered (and quickly) to docile students who receive it. In Blondell and Miller's chapter 6, Diane Gorski struggled with her administrators' message: they felt that students should be engaged in repetitive practice to learn *the* way of writing an essay. In this approach, literature had become something to "cover" and recall, so details could be slotted into state test essays. Her compliant student Natalie read novels, filled out worksheets, took the literature tests, and, she said, "slouched." Diane felt as disempowered as her students: she had experience reading literature aesthetically and reflectively, and this passionate engagement was what she wanted her students to feel and understand. Through the journey by Diane and her students to "meaning that matters," Diane realized her way to becoming "the teacher I'm supposed to be." And her students like Natalie and Kiara learned (finally as 16-year-olds!) what reading literature was all about—the felt, embodied story *and* the possibilities for thematic abstractions, "beyond the literal," about people, lives, times, the world. They moved on—perhaps subversively—to a realm where students made their meanings, learned deeply, *and* passed the state's English Language Arts (ELA) graduation exam.

The trip undertaken by Diane and her students contrasts with other teachers who presumably continued to deliver literature pre-packaged as content superficially covered. For example, another English teacher in the same school and grade level introduced DV composing around student-selected poems, but the teacher listed the "themes" students had to use on the board, disallowed one student's video footage on his cell phone because he had done it outside of school, and ended the project before students finished. Students, in a self-initiated move, completed their videos on their own in the library. The teacher's concern for control of content and movement led her to conclude, "These students can't handle this [activity]" (Miller, 2010).

In light of this traditional-but-obsolete orientation that often predominates within schools, multimodal learning did not just suddenly appear in classrooms. The pre-service and in-service teachers described in this book found supported opportunities to reframe teaching and learning in order to initiate multimodal composing as an effective student-learning tool. In some cases, in-school support for teachers' efforts was useful in helping them reframe their stance towards teaching and learning. Even though students engaged in digital activities outside of school, *they* needed support for multimodal composing in school. Successful teachers designed their pedagogy: it was strategic, orchestrated, planned, nuanced—contingent on the needs of students, their learning (or lack thereof), and on where the teacher both wanted students to go but also sensed that students needed to go. The digital tools offered affordances for learning and composition that were not readily available or accessible before, but the tools were only as good as the learning environments—the classroom spaces negotiated through ongoing interaction.

In this final chapter, we present a cross-case analysis of the chapters. We begin by further exploring tensions as we consider four myths that we feel are challenged by the teachers, students, and practices within the chapters and the research authors have conducted. Second, we return to the model of multimodal literacy practices presented in chapter 8 (Figure 8.2) to further extend and explore a theory of teaching for embodied learning through multimodal composing.

Debunking Myths

These chapters challenge some common myths that have emerged around multimodal composing; these myths reflect many of the tensions articulated above.

Myth #1: Teachers are the major impediment to integrating New and Multimodal Literacies in classrooms. A few teachers had difficulties in expanding their views of literacies and in communicating to students that modes other than print were for decoration. Consider, for example, how Mrs. Bowie in chapter 7 positioned text as the primary mode for carrying information and image as decoration and enhancement. But also consider that unlike many of the teachers discussed in the case studies (e.g., Carol in chapter 2, Joel in chapter 5, Keith in chapter 8), Mrs. Bowie had not had the opportunity to participate in meaningful, ongoing professional development related to multimodal composing. The point here is not that Mrs. Bowie's perspective was more limited than the nuanced understandings exhibited by other teachers, but rather that Mrs. Bowie had not been provided with the same opportunity to learn.

Given that Mrs. Bowie was an enthusiastic teacher who explored new technologies on her own and implemented them within her classroom in ways that extended beyond how they were introduced to her in workshops that stressed operationalized computing, we feel compelled to point out that Mrs. Bowie (the teacher) was *not* the major impediment to her adopting a new stance toward multimodal composing. Rather we suggest that if she had been offered the same opportunities for professional development as other teachers represented here (e.g., Carol, Joel, Diane, and Keith), Mrs. Bowie could have considered her own print-centric stance and implemented a richer conception of multimodal composing. Overall, teachers reported, and we also found, that teachers were constrained more by mandates for test preparation (i.e., school contexts where administrators at all levels demanded only print reading and writing as test preparation).

Myth #2: All students are "digital natives," and teachers as "digital immigrants" are strangers who live by very different "mindsets." Some have argued that students as "digital natives" and teachers as "digital immigrants" live by very different mindsets that are difficult if not impossible to reconcile (Prensky, 2001a,b).[1] We did find that one of the most difficult issues was transforming the views of knowledge into which we (and most teachers of our generation) were socialized during our school experience. Teachers, many who had not grow up in the digital world, did mature and develop in their understandings of multimodal composing. When teachers had high quality professional development and support in classrooms, many expanded their views of literacy and what counts as knowing; they also transformed their pedagogy. With support, teachers in their classrooms enabled multimodal composing across the curriculum. More profoundly, the chapters demonstrate that teachers were essential in mediating students' meaning making and learning.

This second point—that teachers were essential mediators—calls into question the belief that somehow the millennial or post-millennial generation will embrace and engage with multimodal composing intuitively. The cases demonstrate that most students have cell phones/iPods and engage with a variety of media, and clearly many youth engage in numerous digital worlds, but we found that many students did not have much first-hand experience with multimodal composing. This echoes a finding identified by Bennett, Maton, and Kervin (2008) who found that "digital natives" spent most of their time on the Internet gathering information rather than creating it. Consider too, for example, Bruce's (chapter 3) original and incorrect assumption that because students were avid movie watchers, they would be able to use techniques such as camera angles effectively in their multimodal compositions. Bruce learned that students working with multimodal composing needed guidance in "reading and composing." Students did have latent knowledge—consider Abigail and John's use of images in chapter 7—but in the most effective cases, the teachers worked with that knowledge to make knowledge and affordances explicit. Such knowledge became part of a classroom community and classroom practices as teachers strategically cultivated particular practices and learning environments.

In short, both teachers and students are dynamic and can change through engaged social activity and reflection. In the context of multimodal composition, teachers were essential to mediating students' meaning making and learning.

Myth #3: Multimodal composing is extraneous; it takes away from essential class time that should be used for covering basic curriculum and test prep. The pressure in schools to be on the same page as everyone else who was "covering" curricular material was a prevailing tension—that too familiar ghost of education past. But through supported reflection on student learning, teachers felt a fresh agency in their own classrooms, and were ready to support their pedagogical choices with vivid evidence of students' learning. This move *from* feeling/being disrespected (Dudley-Marling, 2005) *to* using professional inquiry and local/global knowledge to support student learning brought teachers a sense of self-respect and efficacy for which they had been yearning (becoming "the teacher I'm supposed to be").

Not only did teachers cover a breadth and depth of material (from science to novels to history), teachers shared multiple stories of students whose school lives and identities were changed: students stopped skipping school to come to class; students stayed after school or over lunch to complete work; students expressed a connection to school and their peers that they had not felt previously; a parent called to report a dramatic change for the better in a child's disposition toward school. To be sure, multimodal composing did take class time, but teachers who successfully integrated multimodal composing *into* their curriculum found that given students' breadth and depth of learning, the time was well spent.

Innovative teachers with support found ways to integrate multimodal composing into their curriculum and still prepare students to pass state tests. Multimodal composing provides embodied experiences (with sights and sounds and movements) that seem to create deep learning and understanding in students, which they carried into timed testing. In the year of the study, to give just one example, Paige and Nicole (Miller, Thompson, Lauricella, Boyd, chapter 8) and all of the students in Keith's classroom, which included mainstreamed special education students, passed the U.S. History graduation exam that featured an essay on multimodal primary source texts such as cartoons, graphs, and photographs (also Lauricella, 2006). While it is true that high-stakes tests most often focus on print literacies, that does not make multimodal composing extraneous.

Myth #4: Multimodal literacies are the opposite of print literacies. The teachers in these chapters worked in urban and suburban schools in elementary, secondary, and higher education. Their teaching experience ranged from 2 to 13 years. Multimodal composing topics ranged from science concepts to historical eras and student-composed "meta-texts" (Miller, 2011, p. 290) that added to and completed poetry, songs, and novels. (See Table 9.1 for a brief summary of participants, activities, and named themes in each chapter.)

As Table 9.1 and each case demonstrates, multimodal literacies are not about choosing new over old, recent over past, or "new and improved" over "old and outdated." The case studies show that print is involved in multimodal composing, during both process and product, and that it can lead back to mediate reading print, as we saw with Natalie and Kiara (chapter 6) or Kimberly (chapter 2), who described how she had to work rereading her print poetry text while she composed a digital poetry interpretation.

Multimodal literacies seek to look at multiple texts—print forms and film, photos, illustrations. These texts are not seen as better or worse, but rather in terms of mode and affordance. In the various classrooms presented here, learners strategize about how modes (e.g., color, movement, sound, etc.) help to communicate and carry meaning within particular social contexts. Alongside this, they consider: What are the affordances or "potentials for making meaning" offered by different modes (Kress, 2009, p. 54)?

Changing the Learning Game with Multimodal Composing: Six Action Principles

In addition to challenging the myths noted above, our cross-case analysis of narratives and findings in chapters showed that the four components for a multimodal literacy pedagogy as introduced in chapter 8 and detailed in Figure 8.2

TABLE 9.1 Teacher and Student Learning and Change through Multimodal Composing

Teacher(s)	*Critical Incident(s) Factor(s)*	*Students*	*Text/Concept*	*Multimodal Text*	*Influence*
McVee, Bailey, Shanahan Ch 2	Transactional perspective; meta-language; computer epiphanies	Deena, Kendra, Jan	Technologies generate new literacies	Poetry interpretation—Powerpoint w/ embedded modes	Teachers treated as learners; opportunities to compose multimodally
David Bruce Ch 3	Video grammar as structural form	Jennifer	Henry VDeconstruction of video scene	Storyboard of existing video	Critical re-reading of video
Carol Smith Ch 4	T-S talk; new literacy stance; local knowledge; explicit attention to design/modes	Lucey, Helena	Narrative Writing; Halloween stories; student-selected poetry interpretation	Print text w/ hyperlinks; Powerpoint w/ embedded modes	T. change to New Literacies stance; S take up multimodal composing
Joel Malley Ch 5	Digital video workshop; S. writing, T-S talk; screenings; New literacies classroom	Mercy, Destiny, Mark	Multimodal composing with student-selected music	Music videos	Thinking & acting, composing like storytellers
Diane Gorski Ch 6	T & S: both need to work with "meaning that matters"	Kiara & Natalie	Novel-*Their Eyes Were Watching God*	Found poem digital video as metatext on novel	T. changed attention to students' meanings; Ss understood thematic abstraction
Mrs. Bowie Ch 7	Designs of meaning; T-S interactions; constrained use of signs	Jeremy & Danielle; Crystal & April; John & Abigail	Acid Rain	Hypertstudio text	T. prioritizes print & visual; S do same, w/ an exception; T. didn't have access to prof develop. on multimodality
Keith Hughes Ch 8	T support at point of need; remixing cultural texts; Ss. lifeworlds; "doing history"	Paige & Nicole	Jim Crow Laws	DV Movie trailer	Deep learning used to read history/world

were reflected throughout these cases. In addition, we determined that these principles were necessary, but not sufficient, to explain the dynamics of the cases. Two other elements recurred in the case-study stories. The components of the reframing of teaching and learning for multimodal composing included, then, six action principles working in synergy.

In the remainder of this chapter we weave together the strands of findings across the cases in order to elaborate the six significant aspects functioning in these classrooms. The principles derived from these research stories work together to manifest *a theory of teaching for embodied learning through multimodal composing*. The six components direct attention to teachers' actions and interactions: teachers' efforts focused on (a) developing a New Literacies stance; (b) initiating a social space for mediation of collaborative composing; (c) co-constructing a sense of felt purpose for students' multimodal composing; (d) drawing on and encouraging students to draw on their identities and lifeworlds; (e) making design elements explicit as meaning-making tools; and (f) supporting embodied learning through students' transmediating symbolically with modes. In what follows, we connect these action principles to the case studies to illustrate their function, each in turn, in the context of classroom use.

Developing a New Literacies Stance

The teachers in this book needed opportunities to engage with multimodal composing, to develop in themselves a first-hand understanding of designing multimodal texts to fuel their support of students in *their* composing efforts. In these activities teachers felt how purpose guided their choices of modes, how drawing on their own knowledge facilitated their composing, and how interacting with others supported their thinking and learning. These experiences embodied in their multimodal activities moved teachers to a new understanding. Conversations during professional development and, in some cases, continued support in and out of classrooms, prompted *teachers, in the best cases, to move into a New Literacies stance*, comprised of new attitudes towards

1. texts (literacy includes print *and* multimodal texts);
2. student knowledge (students need to draw on their experiences to integrate prior knowledge and understanding with curricular "texts"); and
3. student learning (multimodal composing in collaborative spaces generates literacy and learning through embodied inquiry, while also materializing evidence that they occurred).

Teachers' participation in multimodal composing and their reflection on it prompted them to initiate digital composing in their classrooms and to reflect on how better to enact such multimodal composing to engage students and support their learning.

In chapter 2, McVee, Bailey, and Shanahan provided pre- and in-service teachers opportunities to first understand their own multimodal learning in the context of reading, writing and discussing to reflect on new literacies and their own composing experiences. Through this process teachers' concerns arose and were discussed. The teachers moved from the initial flashy novelty or fear of digital technologies to the embodied process of designing texts to represent meaning through multiple modes. Those who were tentative or apprehensive working multimodally and reflecting on the process, over time learned to become comfortable with multimodal practices and with their new positions as collaborators and text composers who did not always know the outcome ahead of time. They were developing new attitudes towards what counts as literacy, student knowing, and the possibilities for learning—a New Literacies stance.

In their classrooms, teachers who attended to and inquired into student learning through multimodal composing became more successful at supporting their students' work. In chapter 4, Bailey traced Carol Olsen's initial use of digital composing as a technology "hook" for learning in traditional literacy practice. Carol had not yet developed a recognition of how literacy and technology can exist together in a more integrated and transactional relationship (McVee, Bailey, & Shanahan, 2008). Through her graduate course readings/discussions and reflections on what was happening with her students, Carol began to realize that multimodality generated through technology should be more than a bait and switch tactic, an anticipatory set for the "real" work with print. She developed new attitudes: "I changed my whole conception of what literacy is."

Her "New Literacies stance" (as Bailey, 2006, coined it) positioned her and students in new ways: using multimodal composing as a social and cultural *literacy* practice, Carol opened opportunities for students to use their "local knowledge" in dialogue and inquiry to construct new meaning. As Carol integrated multimodal composing into her daily instruction, students' participation and activity transformed into identity-making and learning. In the song lyric, Halloween, and music video projects, Carol and her students came to see how using modes thoughtfully *multiplied* meanings, and learned to use modal elements to communicate meaning in powerful new ways, generating intense engagement and literacy learning.

In contrast, Mrs. Bowie (in Shanahan's chapter 7) embarked on multimodal activities without opportunity for her own supported reflection. Her personal interest in engaging her students in 21st-century technologies came from the "technology" professional development in which she had participated. She initiated change by using digital technologies with her students. She did not notice, though, her students' perfunctory use of some modes or her own communicating of a preference for image and print. This story captures a snapshot of Mrs. Bowie and suggests that with more support and/or more reflection on her students' learning, over time she could grow in understanding the use of multimodal signs to represent—that is, as literacies that encoded meaning—not just as technologies. Shanahan captured the moments when Mrs. Bowie was first trying technologies yet had not developed the beliefs and attitudes of a New Literacies stance.

A graduate of professional development on DV composing (Miller, 2007), Diane Gorski (Blondell & Miller, chapter 4) first asked her students to represent elements of an essay rubric as a video ad. She had an almost visceral understanding that this first DV composing assignment did not inspire students as she had hoped, and looked for a new approach that would work "to bring students in." In collaborative opportunities for reflection in project meetings and in her conference presentations, Diane came to see even in that first DV project something she had rarely seen before in her classroom—"student creativity." She noticed that students generated "really good projects" when she provided "less direct assistance," that is, less telling-them-what-to-do.

Reflecting on her own and other teachers' narrated experiences and her own felt engagement in literature, she realized what students needed in order to become invested in their reading, writing, and video composing: what was missing was "meaning that matters" to her students. In later projects, Diane's focus on students using DV composing as a literacy to represent such felt meaning about literature and communicate it, she finally perceived herself as the "teacher I am supposed to be," a teacher who, we would argue, had made a journey that brought her to a New Literacies stance. In this flexible, responsive, adaptive posture, she enhanced her ability to constructively critique her practice and provide support for students at their points of need: in multimodal composing about self-discovery for one of her favorite novels, Diane also found a life-line—"Ok, so this is why I teach. These students were proud of their work and will remember it."

A detail in the story of Diane Gorski's transformation is useful in examining how such change progresses. In her conference presentation, Diane referred to an image of a teacher consulting with a student. In the image from the video, he is squatting down beside a student seated at a computer, her arms across her chest. He looks up at her and she is intently explaining something, a problem maybe. The scene is momentary: he balances himself with one hand on the back of the chair and cannot remain in that position for long. Diane explained to teachers at the conference that she remembered this photograph. She knew the teacher, Keith Hughes, because he was the lead instructor in her professional development institute and this image represented for her, she said, the new position she wanted for herself in her classroom.

The image spoke to her of students' new positions, too. They were composing with print and non-print modes—multimodally—bringing to the conceptual task everything they knew, maybe getting stuck, turning to the teacher and other students to get them moving again. Diane never literally crouched down beside students—it was not her style. But during the found poetry video she did something new—moved around to check in with groups during class.

She did begin each composing workshop with "let me know how I can help you." In short, she used that image to create a framework for what she wanted to become, what she wanted to happen for students in her class. She reflected on her embodied experiences in the DV institute, in professional conversations, and in her classroom until she integrated them into her revised pedagogical frame that represented her intentions to take a New Literacies stance. As teachers moved into their version of a New Literacies stance, they were then able to recruit students into the new game of learning beyond print delivery to individuals.

Initiating a Social Space for Collaborative Work

As a result of their new understandings, teachers were able to initiate a new context for learning by creating spaces for social learning, along with new teacher and student positions as *collaborators in a shared endeavor.* As students took up this invitation to collaborate with the teacher and each other, the classroom often became an *affinity space* (Gee, 2003, 2004) where students sought out all available resources (people, tools, information) to mediate their composing. Students and teachers were both *agents* in this process. Teachers took steps to plan, initiate, and take risks in their teaching, and students took risks, created, and enacted knowledge alongside their teachers.

In chapter 2, the authors (McVee et al.) and their adult students (Janie, Laura, and others) described their own concerns about the distributed knowledge in their classrooms. The teacher-educators shared that they "worried about how students would respond if we did not immediately have an answer" and students (pre- and in-service teachers) offered similar reflections upon their own positions as teachers. Janie observed that "It takes courage and faith in what a project has to offer for a teacher to step down as the expert and embark on a unit that he or she is not completely familiar with." Participants also reflected on their concerns about themselves as learners in a graduate course. Laura described how a classmate had a "higher information salary" than her own when it came to technology—a recognition that somewhat intimidated and inspired Laura. These concerns represent issues that needed to be acknowledged and addressed to create productive social spaces, and teachers took action to effectively create these spaces for collaborative endeavor as students worked side by side to co-construct knowledge.

Talk was essential in this process of socially situated co-construction. Across the chapters, the authors presented clear portraits of classrooms where children talked side-by-side; teachers walked the room to question, suggest, and support; youth shared ideas as they debated the best means of presenting ideas through video, and teachers shared knowledge with their peers. In chapter 7, Shanahan demonstrated through talk the easy rapport that Mrs. Bowie had established with her students as they discussed the role of images and "kid-friendly" text. Shanahan also demonstrated the importance of talk in expressing student knowledge as Danielle and Jeremy considered how to present images that showed that acid rain causes billions of dollars in damage to buildings and other structures. Talk was also a critical mediator for John and Abigail as they designed a representation of the water cycle to show how acid rain could lead to a dead ecosystem.

It might be easy to assume that such talk just naturally happened, but teachers and students in classrooms *made* talk happen. Consider Keith Hughes' description of the spatial layout and classroom design (Miller et al., chapter 8) as a reflection of his multimodal literacy pedagogy. Note how carefully Joel (Cercone, chapter 5) orchestrated the series of activities and actions for his students, and how he invited students to have a voice—"Mercy, the floor is yours." In response Mercy shared her writing about a favorite song, played the song, and presented ideas for a next video. All students described by Cercone referenced how their ideas and voices counted in Joel's classroom. Students discussed ideas with one another and with their teacher to become a "community of writers" who used "social hotspots" as sites to construct, challenge, and explore.

Social mediation, then, allowed for and required challenging tasks that students found meaningful. Often these tasks compelled students (and teachers!) to work together just beyond the capacities they would have demonstrated when working alone (Vygotsky, 1978). These construction sites also reflected the principle that "embodied experience is shaped by others in our social community" (McVee, Dunsmore, & Gavelek, 2005, p. 545).

Co-constructing a Felt Purpose

Across the cases teachers needed to *co-construct with students a felt sense of purpose for multimodal composing.* The purpose was most often bound up in meaning-making for self-expression through representation and communication to an audience. Teachers initiated the purpose in the whole classroom context, especially through the tenor of the assignments and by continually communicating that knowledge and texts needed to be examined, interpreted, and represented for an authentic audience. The framing of the multimodal assignment initiated the purpose for composing as a rhetorical task—representing meaning materially for an audience and oneself.

In chapter 5, Cercone traced the pedagogical practices and influences on students of a savvy tech and literacy teacher. As Joel Malley asked students to read their journal entry on a favorite song, he turned class attention to students' ideas. After several journal readings to which students and Joel responded and asked questions, Joel turned to the assignment that built on their favorite song and journal writing about it: "Your task is to create a conceptual narrative..." And later, "Don't just say something, suggest it as well." This purpose Joel sets is complex, challenging students to orchestrate multiple texts (song lyrics and music, journal writing) through multiple modes available in digital video, composing conceptually—at more than a literal level. To signal what Cercone calls the "DV workshop," Joel set the class in motion with "*Let's go!*"

In the energy and excitement of the "coffee shop-like atmosphere" where students worked, in what Cercone called a "new literacies classroom," Joel persistently focused on each student's ideas and plans during his "daily rounds." Students helped each other, and later Joel asked them to share rough draft video shots and scenes for feedback from their audience—spotlighting whether students' representations met their purpose of communicating conceptually. On the day of the screening, students were visibly excited to share their work, and the first was Mercy's video *I am a Revolution*, which was well received: it "reflects the purposeful consideration of audience and message, of showing instead of telling, and an attention to detail most English teachers would be thrilled to see in their own students' work." Joel's vigorous emphasis on representing and communicating conceptually for an audience was consistently evident and invited students' sense of purpose for multimodal composing in his class.

Keith Hughes (Miller et al., chapter 8) demonstrated that in history class the curriculum content could also engender a strong sense of purpose for multimodal composing. In Keith's class, students engaged in an historical inquiry, first out of curiosity and then out of outrage as they discovered the systemic racism that promoted discrimination and newspaper-advertised lynching of African Americans. Through "doing history," students Paige and Nicole composed a DV whose message progressed into their lives in a variety of ways, prompted by their purpose of making sure their audience knew and understood the history from which they and all Americans have come.

When Mrs. Bowie (Shanahan, chapter 7) focused on using technology, she communicated a purpose for print and image, but not for the other modes; students took up her message and used sound, for example, as ornament, not meaning. When Carol Olsen (Bailey, chapter 4) at first just used multimodality as a "hook" for the real lesson, students soon caught on that these introductions were not purposeful or important. When Carol understood that problem, she co-constructed purpose with students by treating their multimodal composing as a literacy practice with expressive and communicative purpose.

When Diane Gorski (Blondell & Miller, chapter 6) saw that students were not extremely engaged in creating an advertisement on the elements of the state ELA exam rubric (e.g., organization, focus, details, etc.), she was concerned that she was "ruining DV" for her students. The task left little space for students to engage deeply with the curriculum as a multimodal meaning-making practice. Over the course of several weeks, she reframed her perception of DV composing and realized she would have to design a project that had an authentic purpose both for students *and* for learning the curriculum. Diane began to focus the DV activities on literature study through multimodal resources and texts (i.e., performance, song, image, print). She recalled her own DV compositions and attended to her own latent belief that reading print-based texts was a sensory and personal experience: "She considered her own passion for literature [and her favorite novel *Their Eyes Were Watching God*] and realized how she read literature best with all of her senses, through a symbol or a tree or the damp swampland of Janie's muck" (Blondell, 2009, p. 259).

In re-connecting to her belief that reading literature was much more than preparing for the state's timed-essays, Diane also began to re-think the school district mantra of "I do, you do" as the primary pedagogical practice. She saw that this traditional modeling through "imitation" was not conducive to purposeful learning opportunities and realized that, instead, she and her students would have to take on new positions in the classroom. She set up class routines to orchestrate students' action, thinking, and collaboration towards daily goals. In video footage, Diane could be seen circulating and heard asking questions that positioned students as purposeful meaning-makers: "Where do you see your poem going? Where are you taking it?" She saw how her students were committed to their videos, coming in before and after school, during their free or lunch periods. The importance of students' felt purpose was co-constructed by Diane and her students moment-to-moment in the class, a lesson that transformed all of them.

The constant sense of movement we noticed in the reports on these classrooms was not random or chaotic, but focused on the inquiry or representational problem at hand. Their co-constructed purposefulness was the engine for student and teacher activity, agency, and change. Purpose and meaningfulness are necessarily personal and, thereby, require integration of students' selves and understandings into their composing. Drawing on student lifeworlds (lived experience) was another pedagogical principle that emerged from the case stories.

Drawing on Student Identities and Lifeworlds

Encouraging students to *draw on their everyday experiences* (*lifeworlds*) *and identities* allowed them to expand their available resources for making meaning by connecting to what they knew and had experienced, including culturally shaped perspectives. This opening up of the classroom to sources of knowledge outside the textbook and the discipline fueled student attention and interest. Instead of the disciplinary concept being pre-formed and separate from self, it was repositioned as composed *with* self and others in light of inquiry into curriculum and prior knowledge. Making these connections provided another motive for students to engage with multimodal composing—creating coherence in their lifeworld understanding.

In Joel Malley's English class (Cercone, chapter 5), student lifeworlds and narratives were the foundation of their multimodal composing: "Joel frontloaded the assignment by asking students to write about their lives, engaging them in an opportunity to reflect on songs that were important to them. This rooted the work they were doing in terms of their own personal experiences." Drawing on their knowledge of popular culture, students connected traditional forms of written composing with their lived experiences and thinking about music they found significant. Mobilizing their prior experiences and stories in this way connected school with their lives through multimodal composing. Not only do constructed stories of one's identity have "strong emotional resonance," identities are also "a key means through which people care about and care for what is going on around them" (Holland, Lachiocotte, Skinner, & Cain, 1998, p. 5). Students drawing on their lifeworlds emerged as an essential component in many of the case stories, but that did not mean that personal narrative was the only focus.

Students also drew on their everyday experiences with life and media, as they interpreted curricular concepts. Their lifeworlds included experience as consumers/creators of multimodal texts, which formed students' tacit knowledge of multimodal design. David Bruce (chapter 3) depended on this tacit design knowledge in his work with teachers and students in the storyboarding and deconstruction of a video activity. As they looked closely at what Bruce calls "video grammar," they were able to draw on their extensive experiences with movies and TV to make sense of the structural forms in the *Henry V* sequence, re-reading the video to elaborate their understanding of the structure of the multimodal narrative. In chapter 2 (McVee et al.), teachers as learners drew on their latent knowledge of media, also. For example, Deena, Kendra, and Jan made poetry videos on a selected poem as they used multimodal signs to compose meaning about the poem and themselves. In their composing they built on their extensive media experience, eventually linking it to the understanding that computer technologies generate new literacies with the possibility of composing new understanding of self.

Bailey (chapter 4) traced Carol Olsen's emerging understanding that students have well-developed "local knowledge" (Street, 1995) that they could bring to classroom literacy practices. A key change occurred for Carol when she created the poetry video assignment to give students a chance to use their knowledge of music in popular culture to learn poetry, "a bridge between what the students enjoyed and what they needed to learn as the required ninth grade curriculum." Students enthusiastically embarked on an inquiry into the meanings and structures of their own music as a way to understand how poets create poems and how readers create meaning from poems. Bailey describes how "this is exactly what happened."

A consequence of Carol's new appreciation of the local knowledge students had and could use in school was a change in her classroom position from, as she described it, the "high, mighty, authority figure." Students could talk about their selected songs with confidence, a new position that enabled them to lead discussion with peers, connect ideas to other songs, create a poetry interpretation, and use academic discourses (e.g., poetic elements) in new ways for meaning-making.

In a similar way, Diane Gorski's transformation as a teacher (Blondell & Miller, chapter 6) was initiated by her new awareness that school became meaningful to students when they could draw on their lifeworlds. Diane began to answer her question—"How do I give students more control?"—by focusing her attention on student learning. In a "critical juncture," Diane noted how students had knowledge and resources for their composing when she said, she was "relinquishing that control, letting them do things, letting them make decisions, allowing them to discover things for themselves and just being there as a support." She introduced the found poem video assignment on a novel by comparing the process to "what a rapper might do now, or hip hop, what they may call sampling." This cultural activity familiar to students, repositioned them, Blondell and Miller note, "as samplers and interpreters of meaning." After students read aloud their selected lines from the novel, Diane coaxed their thinking and feeling about the character, Janie: "She was 16 [...]that idea of being 16. You guys are about 16, how do you feel? Buzzing, pears, blooming, okay."

Students explored the idea of self-discovery in the novel's words to express an interpretation that was valid and meaningful *to them* and in their videos exceeded Diane's expectations. She saw new agency in students as they got books off the shelf on their own, helped each other, and added Ashanti's song "Don't Let Them" to their video because, for her, it represented Janie's search. Diane found their DVs "amazing" and decided student lifeworlds might be a key: "Maybe we need to tap into the things they do at home, and maybe they'd be more interested in school, and they'd write the essays, and they'd do the thinking that we need 'em to do." Diane provided students opportunity to compose about the literature they had read by connecting the words and representations of the text to their own lives as "16-year olds." A thrilling outcome for Diane was this: "What I've observed from some is that they grew to love the literature in a different way, not just superficially." Such personal influences, learning to love literature read in school, could only develop, we would argue, when students bring themselves and their lifeworlds into their composing.

Students' use of their lifeworld experiences in multimodal composing on curricular texts and concepts provided a transactional influence on students in other cases, too. As they integrated school and their everyday knowledge, they, at the same time, transformed themselves. Mercy, Lucey, Kiara, Natalie, John, Abigail, and the others construed a new sense of self as creative, technologically savvy, and able to understand even difficult texts and concepts. For instance, Paige and Nicole (Miller et al., chapter 8) drew on vernacular history from their community; selected an anti-racist song, "Strange Fruit," suggested by Paige's mother; and enacted scenes about segregation at the school water fountain with a posted sign, "Whites Only." They persuaded a girl to wear a do-rag, and convinced their teacher that they must use the song rather than only a voiceover. This kind of intense meaning-making about the curriculum and drawing from their lives was exactly what the teacher had aimed for in DV composing. He said, "Yes, do it. You have good reasons."

Their finished movie trailer demonstrated the power of students' drawing on community and culture and remixing them with historical images and enacted scenes to communicate their outrage—strong feelings that personally connected them to the curriculum. Using DV to conceptualize their world historically led them to read their world (Friere, 1970/2000) as an historical "text" in which it was no longer acceptable to them that two African American boys should fight over a smudge on a white sneaker—when so much more was palpable to Paige and Nicole in what people "had to go through" to even be in school.

Across the chapters we saw multimodal composing repositioning students in school, in the world, in their own sense of self. Identity is involved in multimodal composing because "the outcome of Designing is new meaning, something through which meaning makers remake themselves" (Cope & Kalantzis, 2000, p. 23). Among the ideas Mercy (Cercone, chapter 5) shared from her journal was this one: "I would like to be great for something." In her video music narrative, she expressed her sense of self, ending with her interpretation of a favorite song: "And be not what looks cool. Be weird, mad, intense, sweet, smart. Be your own you. Day and night." Like Mercy, students in many of these classes learned to conceptualize their lifeworlds, the curriculum and themselves through such composing with multiple modes.

Making Design Knowledge Explicit

Children, students, and teachers interact with and interpret media every day and through this have acquired an awareness of the modes available for design, even if this awareness is latent. This *implicit knowledge* was perhaps best seen in Abigail and John's astute creation of a visual representation of acid rain in a classroom where the teacher continued to privilege linguistic modes over visual modes (Shanahan, chapter 7). To assist students in their composing, teachers needed to *make latent design knowledge explicit*. Students needed to learn the affordances and meaning potential of each mode in the context of their multimodal composing and learn how to design by orchestrating multiple modes to express and communicate meaning.

Many teachers described in this volume observed in themselves this tacit awareness. In chapter 2, Jan pondered this: "Even though I am constantly bombarded with multimedia, I never gave conscious thought to it. I also have never really thought about the multimodal nature of technology." Jan, and the other teachers in her class, learned from their course instructors about multimodality, mode, affordance of mode, and design considerations. They learned to ask: How is meaning constructed? What are the affordances of this mode over that mode? What happens if I layer modes? In situations of supported talk around multimodal text, Jan and her colleagues were introduced to and co-constructed a "metalanguage" (New London Group, 2000, p. 31) or what some have called a "grammar of visual design" (Kress & van Leeuwen, 2006).

As we noted earlier, there is a lot of "doing" in these chapters, but there is also a lot of discussion and knowledge sharing. Time and again, instructors embody what the New London Group (2000) has called "overt instruction." Consider Bruce's careful recounting of his own growing awareness as a teacher as he realized that his students, working with multimodal media, needed support and guidance just as they needed this support and guidance when working with traditional texts. In developing a video grammar, Bruce sought to guide his students and to extend their knowledge even as he provided a means for them to discuss their choices to move beyond "'the liked it/didn't like it' paradigm that often typified discussions of movies." In carefully describing the assignment and presenting examples from student and teacher work, Bruce gives us a first-hand accounting of the planning and supports that teachers must provide to guide student design processes.

In chapter 8, Keith Hughes draws our attention to several considerations of design elements. He describes his classroom space itself as an example of multimodal design. In introducing assignments (e.g., the movie trailer assignment), he assists his students in explorations of particular design elements such as camera angles and shots, lighting, and music. As a history teacher, Keith not only had to attend to his students' creative elements of design as they worked in particular genres (e.g., a movie trailer, an uncommercial), he also had to attend to their interpretations of social studies content. As Miller et al. observed, Keith consistently communicated to his students that digital video composing was "doing history" as students sought to both understand and represent a message related to a particular time period. Keith's explicit, skillful instruction helped students demonstrate a "conscious awareness and control over what is being learned" (New London Group, 2000, p. 33)

This heightened awareness toward multimodality, design, and the affordances of modes was identified by a number of participants. Jan (in chapter 2) commented that "I have even created multimodal products before, but without the metacognitive awareness that I had while creating projects for this class. The projects we did challenged me to think about word meaning, sound, color, layout, genre, and rhythm." Her classmate Laura took deep-seated reflection, design and redesign elements to heart as she created a digital poetry interpretation that demonstrated Kress's proposition that designers work from an intent and reshape resources through recombining modes (see McVee et al., 2008). These same elements appeared in Joel Malley's classroom (chapter 5) as he worked to help students uncover the ways that they matched visual design elements in their videos to the themes, ideas and issues they expressed in their journals and class discussions. The chapter author, Cercone, posits that in so doing Joel helps students to "begin a metacognitive, reflective process."

Bailey, in chapter 4, conveyed this deeper awareness too in presenting Amy's description of a story using hyperlinks and composed in electronic format. Amy explained that she "found the assignment 'harder' than more traditional creative writing assignments" because she was challenged to include hyperlinks in the story. As Amy considered these design modes (e.g., sound, linguistic text), she felt that the hyperlinks actually encouraged writers to use more adjectives. The additional adjectives were a needed element of the design because the linguistic text provided a necessary structure to support the use of audio modes. That is, the affordances of the audio mode were best realized when the linguistic mode was used to set up or design meaning in the most optimal ways.

Making students aware of latent design knowledge required more than just telling them about design. It relied heavily upon shared construction of knowledge and dialogue within social and collaborative spaces, a principle previously discussed in this chapter. Within these spaces teachers and students co-constructed their knowledge of designs, modes, and affordances. This included, as Amy alluded to above, skilled means of thinking and problem-solving to carry meaning across modes and, in particular, to translate meaning from one mode to another—a process discussed below.

Embodied Learning: Transmediating with Symbol-Making Systems

The case study chapters provide evidence of the impact of multimodal composing on students' engagement in school curriculum, on their understanding of disciplinary concepts, and on their robust learning. Why does multimodal composing influence students in these seemingly profound ways? Along with prior scholarship, the case studies provide support for the notion that embodied learning is at work, prompted by the embodied cognition of multimodal composing.

Translating meanings symbolically. In part, these influences come about because during their multimodal composing, students translated meanings from one sign system to another to suit their intended communication. Such purposeful acts of translating meaning from print to images, sounds, and movements across sign systems have been called *transmediating* (Siegel, 1995; Suhor, 1984), as in *moving across media or modes* to represent and communicate meaning. Such transmediating is characteristic of new literacies (Semali & Fueyo, 2001).

The students' composing activities required powerful attention to connect modes of representation (visual, auditory, gestural, spatial)—which are all *human symbol-making systems* (Kalantzis & Cope, 2008). Digital technologies provide ease in creating these associations between symbol systems like image and written text, juxtapositions that provoke and develop thinking (Dickson, 1985). When students link multimodal forms of representation of language, sound, touch, gesture and space, they grow in their literate capacities—their abilities to represent and communicate through symbolically "encoded" texts (Lankshear & Knobel, 2003).

In chapter 4 Bailey followed the change of Carol's perceptions of multimodal composing from a "hook" to grab students' attention to an everyday part of her classroom: as she realized that modes beyond print were literacies that students engaged to materialize their poetry interpretations, she (and her students) came to see the mediation of additional symbolic modes as tools for literacy and understanding. In Shanahan's (chapter 7) narration of the story of a teacher who does not come fully to this understanding, we see students engaged in transmediating concepts on acid rain into images, but other modes were treated as not meaningful, a stance that interrupted the translation process and students' learning. (But even there, one more astute team was able to draw on their media knowledge to transmediate in modes beyond print and image without the teacher's support.)

In chapter 8 (Miller et al.), Paige and Nicole engaged deeply in translating print to multiple modes to represent Jim Crow Laws with music, visuals, and enacted scenes to convey their horror at the planned nature of lynching in this era. They argued together about whether to use the "gruesome" images of lynching and convinced the teacher to let them use Billie Holiday's "Strange Fruit" for part of their sound track—clearly making symbolic translations to represent and communicate powerfully. Their learning was so intense that it provoked them to act jointly against boys ready to fight in the urban school cafeteria—both a historicizing of their lives and an uncommon act of courage in that context.

Simply put, working with meanings at this symbolic level generates deep understanding. What activates this understanding and profound growth is that students are "forming structures or systems of symbol-to-symbol relationships (Kalantzis & Cope, 2008, p. 152). In all, multimodal composing provides multiple modes for transmediating from the print and language of the classroom when students compose new texts that symbolically represent meaning by integrating images, sounds, and movements to re-represent a text or idea.

Embodiment and image schemas. Enacting scenes through movement and gesture in space, selecting music for its tone and theme, creating or capturing images to represent meaning—in each instance, students used their senses, translating print through multiple modes and linking them symbolically. This translation from words to other sensory modes of representation is transmediating, but it is, at the same time, an example of embodied learning.

In chapter 6 (Blondell & Miller), Natalie returned to the novel *Their Eyes*

Were Watching God (Hurston, 1937/2000), to pull out and shape the language that she thought represented Janie's search for love. She went outside the school to film and translated those words into visual images (e.g., leaves of a large tree blowing in the wind) and sounds (the rustle of leaves and music from home) and later overlaid in a bold font, the chosen words to represent Janie's long anticipation, her wait for love. Natalie's translation was an aesthetic experience for her, as she explained about the words and images: "They matched. They matched perfectly."

This embodied composing served as a means of materializing the abstraction winding through the novel about what the teacher called "self-discovery" and what Natalie called "waiting for love." After this experience Natalie understood for the first time, the need to inquire into the meaning of the signs in texts and all around her. Or, as Natalie expressed her learning, "Everything means something." For her this was a new, literate vision of texts in English class. This new conceptual stance, derived from composing meaning from her embodied experience and perceptions of her surroundings, provided Natalie with an expectant view of meaning to be made in the world.

Think back for a moment to the image that her teacher Diane used in guiding her understanding and internalization of a New Literacies stance: The teacher, squatting, balances with one hand on the back of a chair as he looks up at a student seated at a computer. The student's gaze is downward, engaged in discussion with the teacher. Earlier we used this image in articulating a New Literacies stance. Note that we understand "stance"—as Diane did—from an embodied perspective. Wrestlers take a stance. Golfers work to perfect their stance. We understand the metaphor of a New Literacies stance or a teaching stance because the metaphor is grounded in both our physical and conceptual understandings.

New images of teaching promote changed practice through creation and invention, then, not just by acquiring a model, as is. We propose that active conceptual integration of a new pedagogical stance—like the outcomes of students' multimodal composing—cannot be pre-formed and transmitted, but must emerge from the mind and body engaged in generative activity. Perhaps most important here, the integration of such cognitive frames is guided by language, but "it is not inherently linguistic. People manipulate many more frames than they have words and constructions for" (Fauconnier & Turner, 1998, p. 134).

These conceptual integrations, then, occur often beyond words, in what Johnson (1987, 2007) calls an "image-schema," an abstract multimodal mental representation that integrates embodied experience and transforms as a structure and pattern for new experience. While Johnson uses the term "image-schema," readers should note that he is not referring to "schema theory" or related approaches to text processing that many teachers might recall having learned about from their literacy methods texts. Those schema theoretic perspectives draw upon metaphors of the mind as computer or file cabinet—the world is out there, we describe it, categorize it, and file this away as mental knowledge (for a full review see McVee et al., 2005). This perspective contrasts sharply with those scholars we draw on who posit that cognition is an embodied process—the mind as a pattern recognizer in everyday experience. Image schemas, thus, are created by the body and the mind.

This startling idea returns us to the argument for multimodal composing as a tool for learning. If, as some scholars argue, we actively integrate our knowledge into our existing conceptual frames in a process of complex cognition grounded in "bodily experience and feeling" (Johnson, 2007, p. 41), then schooling (including teacher education) must take up these other modes as essential ways of coming to know. "If we think of schema as embodied and not just in the head, then it becomes clear that patterns of enactment, ways of engaging the world, both shape our interpretation of cultural activity and are shaped by cultural activity. This requires very different ways of thinking about teaching and learning" (McVee, et al., 2005, p. 550). In short, we learn through embodied experience, integrating multimodal representations into our conceptual understanding. Across chapters the research stories traced teachers' embodied learning and their efforts to transform their teaching, and traced students' embodied learning in their efforts to represent and understand.

Multimodal Composing Going Forward: Embodied Learning for All

Supporting new and experienced teachers in developing a New Literacies stance requires providing for their embodied learning through multimodal composing, with opportunities for professional conversation and reflection. As these teachers introduce multimodal composing to their students, the continual interplay between thought and action requires this posture of the body and mind that readies a teacher to enact multimodal composing as a powerful literacy and respond flexibly both to students' perceived multimodal literacy problems and to those they do not yet recognize.

The process of enacting multimodal composing, then, is an embodied praxis, requiring teachers to change the classroom game by initiating a social space for themselves and students to engage in pairs or in groups to jointly construct a felt purpose for literacies of representation and communication. By inviting students' identities and lifeworlds into the moment-to-moment interactions and making explicit the communicative potentials of multimodal elements, teachers can support students' efforts to transmediate texts and concepts with modes—and, in those ways, foster students' embodied learning. The case stories provide evidence of teacher and student embodied learning, both, and the identified recurring components provide a theory of teaching for embodied learning through multimodal composing.

The game of learning has changed and *has* to change because the digital world provides easy access to multimodal tools, and cognitive science provides new understanding of how the mind works through multimodal abstractions--the body in the mind (Johnson, 1987). Thereby, the game of teaching must change as well into what we want to call *embodied teaching*—to see, hear, feel, move with student learning. It is not a menu of pedagogical techniques, but a contact activity that requires a New Literacies stance responsive to small moves and nuances at points of need and mediating interactions to sustain the constructing of purpose and composing of meaning by transmediating modes. The integration of body and mind, of curriculum and self, of print and other modes together create embodied learning and teaching in the digital world.

Note

1. Prensky (2001a) introduces the term "digital natives" to refer to those youth who are "native speakers" of the digital language of computers, video games and the Internet (p. 1). In contrast he uses "digital immigrants" to refer to those who did not grow up engaging with these technologies but who came to know them later. As such, immigrants often retain their "accent" and engage in practices that digital natives would never think of (e. g., printing out email to read it). Prensky (2001b) explores evidence from neurobiology, video game studies, and psychology to argue that digital natives think differently and almost certainly have physiological differences in brain structure from digital immigrants. While the metaphor of digital natives versus digital immigrants is a powerful one that gained rapid uptake in educational communities, it is not uncontested. A number of scholars suggest a more critical view and caution against assuming that there are vast learning differences and physiological brain-based differences based on conflicting evidence (e.g., Bennett, Maton, & Kervin, 2008; Helsper & Eynon, 2009).

References

Bailey, N. M. (2006). *Designing social futures: Adolescent literacy in and for new times.* Unpublished doctoral dissertation. University at Buffalo, SUNY.

Bennett, S., Maton, K., & Kervin, L. (2008). The 'digital natives' debate: A critical review of the evidence. *British Journal of Educational Technology, 39*(5), 775–786.

Blondell, M. (2009). *An English teacher's design of digital video composing in an urban high school: Impacts on student engagement and learning.* Unpublished doctoral dissertation, University at Buffalo, SUNY.

Cope, B., & Kalantzis, M. (2000). Multiliteracies: The beginning of an idea. In B. Cope & M. Kalantzis (Eds.), *Multiliteracies: Literacy learning and the design of social futures* (pp. 3–8). London: Routledge.

Dickson, W. P. (1985). Thought-provoking software: Juxtaposing symbol systems. *Educational Researcher, 14*(5), 30–38.

Dudley-Marling, C. (2005). Disrespecting teachers: Troubling developments in reading instruction. *English Education, 37*(4), 272–279.

Fauconnier, G., & Turner, M. (1998). Conceptual Integration Networks, *Cognitive Science, 22*(2), 133–187.

Friere, P. (1970/2000). *Pedagogy of the oppressed.* New York: Continuum Books.

Gee, J. P. (2003). *What video games have to teach us about learning and literacy.* New York: Palgrave Macmillan.

Gee, J. P. (2004). *Situated language and learning: A critique of traditional schooling.* London: Routledge.
Helsper, E., & Eynon, R. (2009). Digital natives: where is the evidence? *British Educational Research Journal, 36*(3), 503–520.
Holland, D., Lachiocotte, W., Skinner, D., & Cain, C. (1998). Identity *and agency in cultural worlds.* Cambridge, MA: Harvard University Press.
Hurston, Z. N. (1937/2000). *Their eyes were watching God.* New York: Harper Collins.
Johnson, M. (1987). *The body in the mind: The bodily basis of meaning, imagination, and reason.* Chicago: University of Chicago Press.
Johnson, M. (2007). *The meaning of the body: Aesthetics of human understanding.* Chicago: University of Chicago Press.
Kalantzis, M., & Cope, B (2008). *New learning: Elements of a science of learning.* Cambridge, UK: Cambridge University Press.
Kress, G. (2009). What is mode? In C. Jewitt (Ed.), *The Routledge handbook of multimodal analysis* (pp. 54–67). New York: Routledge.
Kress, G. R., & van Leeuwen, T. (2006). *Reading images: The grammar of visual design* (2nd ed.). London: Routledge.
Lankshear, C., & Knobel, M. (2003). *New Literacies: Changing knowledge and classroom learning.* Philadelphia: Open University Press.
Lauricella, A. M. (2006). *Digital video production as a tool for learning: Exploring multiple text documents in an urban social studies classroom.* Unpublished doctoral dissertation, University at Buffalo, SUNY.
McVee, M. B., Bailey, N. M., & Shanahan, L. E. (2008). Using digital media to interpret poetry: Spiderman meets Walt Whitman. *Research in the Teaching of English, 43*(2), 112–143.
McVee, M. B., Dunsmore, K., & Gavelek, J. R. (2005). Schema theory revisited. Review *of Educational Research, 75*(4), 531–566.
Miller, S. M. (2007, October). English teacher learning for new times: Digital video composing as multimodal literacy pedagogy. *English Education, 40* (1), 64–83.
Miller, S. M. (2011). Transmediating with multimodal literacies: Adolescent literature learning through digital video composing. In P. J. Dunston & L. B. Gambrell (Eds.), *The 60th Literacy Research Association Yearbook* (pp. 284–298). Oakcreek, WI: Literacy Research Association.
Miller, S. M. (2010, December). *Digital video composing as student learning tool: Findings from a two-year study in urban schools.* Paper presented at the annual conference of the Literacy Research Council, Fort Worth, Texas.
New London Group. (2000). A pedagogy of multiliteracies: Designing social futures. In B. Cope & M. Kalantzis (Eds.), *Multiliteracies: Literacy learning and design of social futures* (pp. 9–37). New York: Routledge.
Prensky, M. (2001a). Digital natives, digital immigrants, Part 1. *On the Horizon, 9*(5), 1–6.
Prensky, M. (2001b). Digital natives, digital immigrants, Part II: Do they really think differently? *On the Horizon, 9*(6), 1–9.
Semali, L., & Fueyo, J. (2001, December/January). Transmediation as a metaphor for new literacies in multimedia classrooms. *Reading Online, 5*(5). Retrieved from: http://www.readingonline.org/newliteracies/lit_index.asp?HREF=semali2/index.html
Siegel, M. (1995). More than words: The generative power of transmediation for learning. *Canadian Journal of Education, 20*(4), 455–475.
Street, B. (1995). *Social literacies: Critical approaches to literacy development, ethnography, and education.* Boston, MA: Addison-Wesley.
Suhor, C. (1984). Towards a semiotics-based curriculum. *Journal of Curriculum Studies, 16,* 247–257.
Vygotsky, L. S. (1978). *Mind in society: The development of higher psychological processes* Cambridge, MA: Harvard University Press.

ABOUT THE CONTRIBUTORS

Nancy M. Bailey is an assistant professor in the department of Adolescent Education at Canisius College in Buffalo, New York, where she teaches courses in adolescent literacies and secondary English methods. Dr. Bailey's primary research interests are new literacies and teacher education.

Monica Blondell teaches in the Department of Reading and Academic Success at Jefferson Community and Technical College. She earned her doctoral degree at the University at Buffalo/SUNY while Assistant Director of City Voices, City Visions. Dr. Blondell's ethnographic dissertation examined how an English teacher integrated digital video composing into her classroom. Dr. Blondell's research interests are teacher development and multimodal composing.

Fenice B. Boyd is Associate Dean for Teacher Education and associate professor of Literacy Education in the Graduate School of Education, University at Buffalo/SUNY. Her research focuses on issues of diversity as it relates to students' ethnic, cultural, and linguistic backgrounds, academic abilities, instructional approaches, and curriculum materials. She has published numerous journal articles and a co-authored book, *Principled Practices for Adolescent Literacy: A Framework for Instruction and Policy* (2006).

David L. Bruce, Ph.D., is an associate professor of English Education at the University at Buffalo/SUNY. His research and teaching interests deal with students composing with Digital Video (DV) technology in classroom contexts, incorporating multimodal literacies into teacher education, and exploring uses of DV as a research tool.

James Cercone teaches English Education courses at the University at Buffalo/SUNY. Dr. Cercone's research interests include teaching and learning in diverse urban and first-ring suburban classrooms, sociocultural perspectives on learning, New Literacy Studies, and the development of professional social networks to support teacher growth. His dissertation, a year-long ethnographic study, examined students' literacy practices and their teacher's approach to instruction in an English digital video composing course.

Ann Marie Lauricella, Ph.D., is an assistant professor of education at the State University of New York at Geneseo, where she teaches courses in social studies methods, social foundations, and multicultural education. Her research centers on using technology to promote deep understanding of historical topics that focus on social justice, historiography, and the evolving American narrative.

Lynn E. Shanahan, Ph.D., is an assistant professor of literacy at the University at Buffalo/SUNY where she teaches courses in elementary literacy methods and assessment. The focus of her research is composition of multimodal texts with digital technologies and the use of digital video as a mediational tool in teacher education.

Mary K. Thompson, Ph.D., is a former assistant professor at the University at Buffalo/SUNY. Her research examines multimodal literacies in online spaces. In her work as a consultant in the Chicago area schools, Thompson looks at professional development of teachers in multimodal literacies and publishes curricula that incorporate multimodal literacies into everyday student practices across the contents. Currently at the University of Wisconsin-Madison, Thompson works with faculty, residents, and fellowship programs to ensure competencies are met across program areas.

CONTRIBUTING EDITORS

Mary B. McVee is an associate professor of Literacy Education and Director of CLaRI (Center for Literacy and Reading Instruction) at the University at Buffalo/SUNY. Her work focuses on supporting teachers' and teacher educators' explorations of diversities in digital technologies and multimodality and diversities in relation to culture. Professor McVee brings these two areas together through an interest in narrative, both digital narrative and personal spoken or written narrative and poetry. In addition to other journals, her work has appeared in the *Review of Educational Research, Research in the Teaching of English, Teaching and Teacher Education, Narrative Inquiry, and Teaching Education*. Her most recent book with Cynthia Brock and Jocelyn Glazier (2011) is *Sociocultural Positionings in Literacy Research: Exploring Discourse, Culture, Narrative, and Power.*

A former English teacher and current national leader in English Education, **Suzanne M. Miller** studies how literacy practices in the digital world change teaching and learning. She is Director of the City Voices, City Visions (CVCV) Digital Video Composing project, which prepares teachers to bring students' understanding of digital media into school as a learning tool. Funded by grants from New York State Education Department and private foundations, CVCV has been named by PBS as one of the top five media projects in the United States. Miller's research on this topic garnered the 2007 Janet Emig Award for best journal article in *English Education*. She has published her research in two books and numerous journals, including *American Educational Research Journal, Research in the Teaching of English, Literacy Research Association Yearbook, Theory and Practice in Social Education, Contemporary Issues in Technology and Teacher Education, English Quarterly, English Journal*, and *English Leadership Quarterly*. In 2008 Miller received the Rewey Belle Inglis Award for Outstanding Woman in the Teaching of English, from the National Council of Teachers of English.

INDEX

Page numbers in *italics* indicate figures and tables.